The AUTHORITY ADVANTAGE

PABLOS —

Welcome to the Forbes Books
Family :)

The AUTHORITY ADVANTAGE

BUILDING

THOUGHT

LEADERSHIP

FOCUSED ON

IMPACT

NOT EGO

ADAM WITTY & RUSTY SHELTON

Forbes | Books

Published by Forbes Books, Charleston, South Carolina.
Member of Advantage Media.

Forbes Books is a registered trademark, and the Forbes Books colophon is a trademark of Forbes Media, LLC.

Printed in the United States of America.

10 9 8 7 6 5 4 3 2 1

ISBN: 978-1-95588-486-0 (Hardcover)
ISBN: 978-1-95588-487-7 (eBook)

LCCN: 2022920717

Cover design by Matthew Morse.
Layout design by Wesley Strickland.

This custom publication is intended to provide accurate information and the opinions of the author in regard to the subject matter covered. It is sold with the understanding that the publisher, Forbes Books, is not engaged in rendering legal, financial, or professional services of any kind. If legal advice or other expert assistance is required, the reader is advised to seek the services of a competent professional.

Since 1917, Forbes has remained steadfast in its mission to serve as the defining voice of entrepreneurial capitalism. Forbes Books, launched in 2016 through a partnership with Advantage Media, furthers that aim by helping business and thought leaders bring their stories, passion, and knowledge to the forefront in custom books. Opinions expressed by Forbes Books authors are their own. To be considered for publication, please visit **books.Forbes.com**.

ADAM WITTY

For entrepreneurs: creators, idea makers, and innovators who have so much to share with the world.

RUSTY SHELTON

To my wife, Paige, whom I love more than any words on a page could express. Thanks for inspiring, pushing, and supporting me. Life is so fun and rewarding with you. To my children, Luke, Brady, and Sadie, who bring so much joy to my life and make me the proudest dad in the world. To my parents, Walt and Roxanne, and my sister, Courtney, for the rock-solid foundation of support. And to each and every mentor, partner, and team member I've had the pleasure to build brands with up to this point.
We're just getting started.

A WELCOME GIFT

Download Adam and Rusty's e-book, *Authority Marketing*, for free. In this book, you will explore the seven foundational pillars of Authority Marketing, including why thought leadership is your most important secret weapon to grow business, attract opportunity, and make competition irrelevant.

OUR FRESHEST INSIGHTS

Access the best tools and ideas for leaders who want to build authority in their field on our blog.

TAKE THE ASSESSMENT

Find out your Authority Status: Are you sought after for your expertise, an influencer for leaders in your field, or a novice looking to expand your reach?

OTHER RESOURCES

- *The Definitive Guide to Publishing Your First Book: For Entrepreneurs, Business Moguls, and CEOs* clearly and carefully explains the book publishing process for professionals.
- *Our Welcome Guide* outlines everything you want to know about Authority Media and Publishing Programs at Forbes Books plus how-to articles and examples of more than fifteen authors who have leveraged a book to open doors and build their Authority.

APPLY TO BE OUR NEXT FORBES BOOKS AUTHOR

Forbes Books is for leaders who truly are the best in business in their field and want to share their knowledge and passion to make an impact. Join an exclusive community limited to those who apply and meet certain criteria and elevate your success to significance. **BOOKS.FORBES.COM/APPLY**

GET IN TOUCH

Call us at **843-414-5600** or email us at **INFO@FORBESBOOKS.COM**

WE WISH YOU ALL THE BEST ON YOUR JOURNEY TO CONTINUED SUCCESS!

For current resources, visit our website at:
BOOKS.FORBES.COM/AUTHORITY-RESOURCES

CONTENTS

FOREWORD

I WAS FIRED. SACKED. My ideas were too radical for my new bosses at the large, famous company where I had been vice president of marketing. That was twenty years ago.

Without a job, I immediately began building authority by creating a website and email newsletter. I started my blog soon after, and it is still going strong today. And I started speaking at conferences and events.

However, the most important thing I did to build an Authority Advantage was write books. My international bestseller *The New Rules of Marketing and PR*, originally published in 2007, is now in an eighth edition and has sold nearly a half million copies in twenty-nine languages from Albanian to Vietnamese. I've written thirteen books (so far), and several of them made the *Wall Street Journal* best-seller list. One of my books, *Marketing the Moon,* was even adapted for the three-part PBS American Experience miniseries called *Chasing the Moon.* How cool is that?

To say that the authority I've built has changed my life would be a massive understatement!

The Authority Advantage I created from my books and online content allowed me to exit the corporate world gracefully and live a life of passion. It's allowed me to serve tens of thousands of people, helping them to grow their businesses and be more personally fulfilled. And, yes—the Authority Advantage I've built also means I'm making way more money than I did working for big companies.

An Authority Advantage works so well that it feels like cheating!

This is especially true as consumers have become more and more skeptical of companies, people, and brands.

Everyone is skeptical today. Your team. Your customers. Your suppliers. Your partners. Heck, even your neighbors!

We're skeptical of the teenage TikTok influencer selling clothing on her channel. We're skeptical of the big company that says it cares about the environment. And we're skeptical of the CEO who talks about customers being the most important constituent they serve.

The good news is that skepticism melts away when you create an Authority Advantage by authentically positioning yourself as the mission-driven leader you are.

As my friend Seth Godin likes to say, "Leadership matters." And the kind of leadership that matters most in this environment is the visible kind—the kind that can build affinity with an increasingly skeptical audience.

Visible leadership is the most effective form of marketing today. It allows you to influence people before you directly interact with them.

Fortunately, you are digging into a book that will show you how to create the most important advantage that exists today—the ability to create trust in a distrusting world.

As Adam and Rusty will show you in the pages to follow, creating an Authority Advantage doesn't happen by accident. Instead, it's a systematic approach, a shift from being seen as simply having something to sell to becoming a thought leader having something to teach.

I've known Adam and Rusty for more than a decade and admire the businesses they've built that are a result of both their authority as well as their helping others create their own authority.

When done well, authority isn't about ego. It's about impact and trust, and it's the most important thing leaders can do to serve.

I wish this book had been available to me twenty years ago when I was trying to figure out how to create an Authority Advantage. The good news is, you're reading it now—so you are on the fast track to building the kind of authority that will change your business and your life!

DAVID MEERMAN SCOTT
Business growth strategist and author of twelve books, including
The New Rules of Marketing and PR
www.DavidMeermanScott.com
@dmscott

THE URGENCY OF THE AUTHORITY ADVANTAGE

THERE IS NO DOUBT what the most important currency in business and in life is: trust.

Nothing of meaning happens without it.

There is nothing groundbreaking about this timeless, universal truth. What's new in today's environment is that everything has changed about the way trust is built.

We no longer trust the institutions, organizations, and corporations that once enjoyed this very trust as a foregone conclusion.

As a leader, it's likely you have sensed this shift for some time, including the way you personally view messages you hear from the entities you interact with, be they governmental organizations, companies, media outlets, educational institutions, or even nonprofits. You may not be fully aware of the enormity of the challenge this presents as you steer your organization into the future.

This growing distrust of entities has been gaining momentum for some time. It's more difficult to pinpoint where the shift began than when it became complete. The COVID-19 pandemic was the final blow to trust in an already skeptical world, cementing distrust toward the entities that had enjoyed an ingrained trust for generations.

As a result, leaders can no longer rely on the "brand" of their organization or even their title to inspire trust with stakeholders.

> **LEADERS CAN NO LONGER RELY ON THE "BRAND" OF THEIR ORGANIZATION OR EVEN THEIR TITLE TO INSPIRE TRUST WITH STAKEHOLDERS.**

This shift creates an enormous quandary for leaders who find themselves challenged and perhaps even overwhelmed by the enormity of this transition—particularly those who have shied away from any level of personal visibility beyond their teams up to this point.

How can leaders step up to build trust in this postinstitutional environment?

By leading out front instead of from behind.

Let us share a secret: although your target audience may no longer trust your company, they are still willing to trust *you*.

In fact, they are actively looking for leaders who are authentic, effective, mission driven, and—crucially in today's landscape—visible.

It's not enough to be authentic, effective, and mission driven behind the scenes, because it confines the impact a leader can have to only those who are directly connected with them. This stunts the impact of that leader on an organization that now needs them to be the trust "on-ramp" more than ever.

This new reality is a shock to the system for servant leaders. For years these leaders have been told to serve others and grow their organization from a less visible vantage point.

Today, the less visible you are as a leader, the less you serve those around you, be they team members, customers, or those who can be positively impacted by your message.

People can't trust leaders they don't know. If you're leading behind the scenes or behind the corporate brand, you are likely less effective. The only people who know (and hopefully trust) you are those who deal with you directly in a boardroom, team meeting, or in-person setting.

Today, servant leadership requires leaders to flip a key tenet of the previous servant leadership model. Rather than serving behind the scenes, serve out front as the starting point in building trust with people inside and outside your organization.

We wrote this book as a wake-up call and road map for the kind of leaders we identify with—humble, servant minded, and focused on executing for the good of their customers, teams, and partners. If you identify as this kind of leader, you've probably avoided any limelight personally because you have told yourself you are too busy or you were worried that visibility might come across the wrong way (hint: ego trip).

This well-meaning but dated leadership mindset is preventing you from recognizing that your lack of authentic, mission-driven visibility is costing you and your organization dearly.

The good news is that you picked up the perfect leadership book for this environment.

For more than two decades, we have been helping the world's most influential leaders create an Authority Advantage to grow their organizations and make a bigger impact. We believe our framework has never been more important than it is today.

As entities and leaders finally wake up to the importance of building individual authority or thought leadership, many will do it the wrong way and spoil a golden opportunity to create an unfair advantage in this marketplace.

We want to do two things with this book:

1. Encourage you to create an Authority Advantage and show you how to do it so you can serve those around you.

2. Prevent you from wasting time, money, and goodwill by doing it the wrong way.

So why worry about creating an Authority Advantage in the first place? Can't you just keep doing the things that got you to this point?

We absolutely want you to keep doing all the great things you do so well behind the scenes as a leader. But if you want to create an advantage in today's marketplace, you must shift your visibility beyond your team.

Let's go back to the singular focus of this book: creating trust in a distrusting world.

As you likely learned early in your career, before you can effectively lead, you must create trust.

Trust is the foundation for every single relationship you have—whether it is personal or business. We realize that we're not breaking any news with that reminder; every leader knows that any good relationship starts by building trust.

Yet where most leaders miss the mark is not a lack of awareness about the importance of trust but rather a misunderstanding of how and when to establish it.

In the past, trust was built primarily in person, over the phone, or as a result of a great experience doing business together.

Today, trust is cemented over the long term based on the relationship and/or a job well done. However, the conditions for trust are actually created far before you ever come in contact with someone for the first time. This is true for potential employees, clients, partners, stakeholders, or anyone else thinking about taking a first step with you.

Before you earn a chance to make an impression and build trust in person, you must create a connection and build trust from afar—beginning online.

Do you have any idea what kind of impression you are making right now?

In our experience, most leaders don't.

That's why we wrote this book. We want you to understand that the cornerstone for building trust and creating a connection isn't your business brand—it's *you*, particularly once you create your Authority Advantage.

As we mentioned earlier, COVID-19 accelerated a shift that was already underway—we don't trust institutions, corporations, or entities of any kind in the way we once did. In the postlockdown landscape, we apply a mental filter to every piece of information we consume: *Who created this? What is their agenda? What are they trying to get me to do? Can I trust them? What do they have to gain?*

If the information we are receiving is coming from an institution, company, or other entity, we trust it far less than we do information coming from an individual or leader. This is creating significant challenges for any organization looking to communicate with an audience such as constituents, viewers, stakeholders, current or potential employees, current or potential customers, or anyone else.

Many leaders have been so focused on trying to keep their companies afloat financially through the pandemic that they haven't realized the urgency with which their leadership and broader marketing and media strategies must change. This shift is creating an inner dialogue for leaders about whether or not they need to take a step forward and remove barriers to their audience by creating a personal brand—especially those who, up until now, have vigorously avoided any sliver of personal visibility and have fallen behind as a result.

Does that sound familiar?

Owning the first impression around your brand isn't enough in today's environment—you must remove as many barriers as possible between you and your audience.

In the pages to come, we're going to show you why it's an absolute must to not only be intentional about your personal brand as a leader but also to own your media and, therefore, the connection to your audience. Don't make the mistake of leaving your ability to communicate with that audience up to the benevolence of others, such as social media platforms like Facebook and LinkedIn or earned media gatekeepers like producers, journalists, or meeting planners. *You* need to be in control, not them.

Before you can grow an audience, you must earn their attention and trust with the right approach. That is what this book is all about.

You may not have been prepared for the COVID-19 pandemic by having a great personal brand or a large digital footprint already in place, but you can still create an advantage for yourself in this new media environment—something that will change everything about your reach and influence as a leader.

As you are about to learn, building authority isn't an exercise in ego when done correctly—it's an investment in making an impact at a much larger scale. Here's what it comes down to: building your Authority Advantage is about positioning yourself as a leader with something to teach rather than as an "operator" with something to sell.

Before we go any further, you might be asking yourself, "Who exactly are Adam Witty and Rusty Shelton? And why should I listen to them?"

Building authority for CEOs, entrepreneurs, and leaders who want to make a positive impact has been our life's work.

With forty years of combined experience in this field, we've helped over twenty-five hundred leaders strategically and systematically create their own media (books, podcasts, newsletters, etc.) to build

BUILDING YOUR AUTHORITY ADVANTAGE IS ABOUT POSITIONING YOURSELF AS A LEADER WITH SOMETHING TO TEACH RATHER THAN AS AN "OPERATOR" WITH SOMETHING TO SELL.

an audience and become the go-to guy or gal in their field while expanding the impact of their message to build trust at scale.

In 2005, Adam founded what is today Forbes Books, the book publishing brand of Forbes Media, publisher of *Forbes* magazine. Rusty founded his first agency in 2010, and in 2016 we joined forces because we complemented each other's strengths so well. Adam's specialty is content creation and book publishing. Rusty is a successful entrepreneur and an expert in digital media and public relations, founding his newest agency, Zilker Media, in 2017. Between the two of us, we've written seven books and spoken to audiences around the globe, from Harvard Medical School to YPO (formerly Young Presidents' Organization) and Entrepreneurs' Organization chapters. We also host our own podcast and have been featured in the *Wall Street Journal, Investor's Business Daily, USA Today,* FOX News, and the ABC network, as well as many others.

Together we have worked with more than a hundred *New York Times* and *Wall Street Journal* best-selling authors and a few self-made billionaires as well as CEOs of NYSE- and NASDAQ-listed publicly traded companies. And throughout this book, you'll hear from prominent thought leaders on what they have learned as they created an Authority Advantage.

In short, helping the world's best leaders expand their impact and build authority is what we are all about. We want to add you to that list after you read this book.

As you continue through these pages, we are going to share a step-by-step road map for creating an Authority Advantage for your business, your legacy, and your life. First, however, we're going to start by understanding the big shifts that are driving this new climate and why an Authority Advantage is more an urgent essential than a nice-to-have for today's leaders.

PART ONE

WHY MAKE THIS JOURNEY?

*WHY IMPACT-DRIVEN LEADERS NEED
AN AUTHORITY ADVANTAGE*

1

WHAT IS THE AUTHORITY ADVANTAGE?

PATTI BRENNAN IS one of the most respected financial advisors in the country, ranking near the top of Barron's annual list of top advisors year after year. As CEO of Key Financial Inc., she excels in wealth management for high-net-worth individuals and is ranked as the number one Best-In-State Wealth Advisor by *Forbes*. Her company is among the top female-owned advisory firms in terms of assets under management. This is a leader who has risen to the absolute top of her field with so much to teach in her topic area.

And yet, she was reluctant to lean into building an Authority Advantage when she first came across the framework.

She viewed thought leadership and personal branding as "egotistical," and to be honest, it turned her stomach a little. It felt like bragging to her, and, as for most impact-driven leaders, that's not something she likes to engage in.

Maybe you've had the same reaction to those suggesting you position yourself as an authority in your field. If so, we get it. We find that's the case for a lot of leaders when they consider the idea.

We ask you to reflect on just why you might be having that knee-jerk reaction.

The most common and obvious reason is that your thoughts probably go to people you see doing this the wrong way. They are building a "Hey, look at me!" kind of brand that comes across as more of an ego trip than an impact-driven initiative.

There are plenty of examples of attempted "brand building" gone wrong. These examples, which can litter your LinkedIn, Facebook, or Instagram feeds, often give leaders the wrong impression that to build thought leadership, you have to do it *that* way—by proclaiming your "greatness" in an obvious and even obnoxious way.

You don't have to do it that way—and you shouldn't if you want to build trust.

Let's make this clear at the start of this book: when we encourage you to create your Authority Advantage, we're not interested in stroking your ego.

Many leaders have the mistaken impression that building their brand in a more public-facing way runs counter to the servant leadership model they have been successful with and take pride in. If we had a dollar for every time we've heard a well-meaning leader say, "I'm worried my colleagues will think I'm doing this for the wrong reasons," we'd be competing for a top spot on the coveted Forbes 400 list.

Good leaders remove friction from their teams. They address anything getting in their way and empower them to be successful in their roles in the most fulfilling and impactful way possible.

Good leaders who are winning today understand that their best and highest service isn't limited to those who are already a part of the business—it includes building trust and rapport with *potential* customers, partners, and team members at scale. If a leader isn't providing value in a public-facing way, they limit the impact they have on the business they lead. As a result, they do their existing team a disservice.

Building your Authority Advantage is the complete opposite of building a brand about you. We want you to *be the messenger, not the message!*

Consider servant leadership, something many of us aspire to embody as much as possible. Being a servant leader is about serving others in the same way that being a mission-driven authority is about serving others. The difference is that mission-driven thought leadership expands your reach and impact to those who aren't fortunate enough to have a chance to interact directly with you, allowing you to reach and build trust with far more people.

This is how Patti Brennan, who originally shied away from the spotlight but is now regularly featured in national media, came to see the wisdom of the Authority Advantage:

> I realized that if people in our community, or even in our nation, don't know that we exist, or they don't know who to call, they may call someone who does not have the depth of knowledge or experience, or they may be calling a salesperson who does not have their best interest at heart. Then everyone loses—especially the client and their family.

In other words, building mission-driven authority is an important foundation of modern servant leadership because you extend your impact at scale. This is something we're going to explore in more detail as we unpack the Authority Matrix later in this section.

BUILDING MISSION-DRIVEN AUTHORITY IS AN IMPORTANT FOUNDATION OF MODERN SERVANT LEADERSHIP BECAUSE YOU EXTEND YOUR IMPACT AT SCALE.

But first, you should know that an Authority Advantage carries with it a special bonus.

In addition to making a bigger impact, you position yourself to build your business by creating influence and leverage at a scale you can't imagine.

Whatever you may think about building visibility or a personal brand, the reality is, leaders who build authority give themselves a distinct advantage over all others in the marketplace and make a far bigger impact than those who don't. Those who continue to try to build trust in the marketplace through their corporate brand are going to fall further and further behind as their audience moves further away from institutions.

Unfortunately, this is the default for most leaders: to try to build visibility by leading with their organization's brand. This limits the reach of any message because their audience has a distrusting mindset with entities. This reluctance to elevate their visibility keeps them from making the impact they desire—and limits their understanding of how important their personal brand is to their ability to grow their business and build trust with an increasingly skeptical marketplace.

If you share this reluctance, our guess is that it's prevented you from going down this road—until now.

Finally, let's address the other elephant in the room—time.

We know.

Your plate is already full, and the thought of adding additional items to your to-do list is probably something that generates pangs of anxiety and dread. You may have even felt a jolt of that as you picked this book up—one more thing to do.

This is a fair point and one we understand very well. The mere thought of creating more content or wading into the management of social media can be overwhelming for even the most experienced content marketer—and that's before you think about authoring a book, hosting a podcast, writing a column for your industry's top trade publication, or pursuing some of the other avenues that we'll talk about in this book to expand the impact of your message and build trust at scale.

Through the Master Authority Plan (MAP) we're going to help you build, the process will be customized to your time and goals and will show you the difference between unproductive activity and results-driven strategies as we focus on the best and highest use of your time. We want you to find the quickest route between point A and point B and to have as much fun as possible along the way.

This book is not about getting famous. In fact, it's not even about personal branding. This book is about a mindset shift that will give you, your team, and your company a competitive advantage in a crowded, noisy business environment—simply by building trust.

We believe the greatest force for good in the world is entrepreneurship, and we wrote this book to help founders and leaders cut through the clutter and build a focused, proven plan to grow thought leadership, create leverage, and make a bigger impact in a new landscape.

We're going to zoom out before zooming in. We will start by describing the big shifts underway in the global landscape and setting out why there is an urgency for you to plant a flag for your message as soon as possible. From there we'll transition into a deep dive on building your brand in a way that is authentic to you and your message. We'll focus on building trust with those who don't yet know you—before you have had any engagement with them whatsoever. We'll wrap up in our final section with a "lay of the land" by examining the postmedia landscape; unpacking rented, earned, and owned media; and showing you why each must be integrated with an emphasis on "owning" the relationship with your audience.

But most importantly, this book is meant to empower you.

We want you to control your own destiny and provide outsized value to those around you, such as customers, partners, team members, or those who should be working with you. Our goal is to demystify the topic of thought leadership that for so long has been opaque and overwhelming. When done correctly, it creates a shift that changes everything—and that defines the Authority Advantage.

Let's get started.

2

THE BIG SHIFTS

HOW MUCH HAS your life as a leader changed since the start of the COVID-19 pandemic? Regardless of whether or not your business is booming or struggling, our guess is that you have been challenged as a leader in ways you never thought possible.

We certainly have.

It's amazing looking back on the pandemic and how much changed in such a short time. Although it feels like a lifetime ago, it was early February of 2020 when our team gathered for our Q2 2020 planning session.

As we always do for our planning process, we built a list of important issues to discuss to ensure we landed on the best possible plan for the quarter. We compiled about fifteen issues, and the room went a bit silent as we looked around to see if anyone had anything else. Someone timidly (and, it turns out, prophetically) asked, "Do you think we should talk about this virus?"

At that point it honestly felt a bit silly to be discussing a little-known virus that was half a world away as a potential variable for Q2 of our business. It was just starting to appear in the United States and was still widely considered to be a mild threat. We discussed it but left the meeting writing it off as a long shot in terms of impacting business.

COVID-19, of course, went from a passing thought to the number one issue the world has faced in the past seventy-five years. It not only changed just about everything about the way business is conducted but, more broadly, how life is lived. It is often said that "change is the law of life," but there has never been something that changed the modern business world more quickly and abruptly than COVID-19.

Even as the world of work has come back to life, business travel is often now done between rooms at your house. In-person meetings are now done via Zoom (also RIP phone calls). Purchases of almost every kind are made online. Flexible work arrangements are now a standard expectation for many desirable job candidates.

There have been winners, and there have been losers. Some of those winners were just plain lucky (owning a bike shop instead of a restaurant or an at-home fitness equipment company instead of a gym). Others who came out on top were ahead of the curve before the pandemic because they had already built a brand that people trust. But across the board, all business leaders have been challenged in ways they never thought possible.

We used to wonder if our generation would ever have to deal with a seismic challenge the way older generations have, with disruptions like the Great Depression and World Wars I and II.

To be frank, prior to the pandemic, we had it pretty easy as leaders, avoiding difficult large-scale disruption. Sure, we had 9/11 and the Great Recession, but nothing that could have prepared us for the disruptions caused by COVID-19.

The true enormity of the tragedy is still being felt by millions of families who lost loved ones around the world. But the pandemic also caused a great reset for every fabric of our lives, including the way business gets done. The shifts have been seismic, from the changing realities and expectations about remote work to the enormous challenges impacting supply chains, talent management, and inflation.

As if these challenges weren't enough, leaders are also dealing with a shift that was already underway prior to the pandemic but is now a runaway train—the loss of trust. Trust in institutions is at an all-time low, according to the global consultancy firm Gallup. Averaged out, only 27 percent of US adults express "a great deal" or "quite a lot" of confidence in the fourteen institutions Gallup measures each year, which include the media, our government, the big banks, etc.[1] That's the lowest number Gallup has ever recorded for this poll.

This stat forms the foundation for the first distrust mindset your audience has for your company, institution, or entity, which is the primary reason for the cattle prod of urgency that we're sticking you with early in this book.

What does that number tell us? In today's landscape, the best way to truly communicate a message isn't through a government, company, or entity. Instead, the quickest and most reliable route is to do it through a trustworthy, strategically visible leader.

---

1   Jeffrey M. Jones, "Confidence in U.S. Institutions Down; Average at New Low," *Gallup News*, July 5, 2022, https://news.gallup.com/poll/394283/confidence-institutions-down-average-new-low.aspx.

Think of the power of Volodymyr Zelenskyy's remarkable leadership as the president of Ukraine. His charismatic and genuine personality not only galvanized his own people to fight back against the Russian invasion in 2022 but also motivated much of the international community to back Ukraine's efforts. He did that through a strategic and frequent use of social media and video conferencing in order to create trust and inspire action among his people—and the world. His visibility gave a face to Ukraine that allowed people all over the world to bond with his leadership.

While visible, authentic, and transformational global leaders like Zelenskyy—or even Churchill or Roosevelt—made an impact at a far greater geopolitical level, the same principles apply to every entity.

Think about this remarkable difference between businesses that have a well-known, authentic public-facing leader and those who don't. It creates a seismic advantage in today's landscape when that leader focuses their energy on connecting with stakeholders in an authentic, valuable, and visible way. Are you giving your business a similar advantage?

As you think about the answer to that question, let's dig deeper on the three seismic shifts driving much of the urgency of this book.

SHIFT 1: FROM CORPORATE BRANDING TO AUTHORITY BRANDING

Most entrepreneurs and leaders are conditioned to focus all marketing and branding efforts on one thing: building the corporate brand. This strategy is often based on one of two misguided notions:

1. The value of an institution is more sustainable over time if it isn't built on the reputation or personality of any one person.

2. Attempting to build both a corporate brand *and* a leader's brand creates conflict and ultimately dilutes both.

Both are fallacies that cause significant pain for entrepreneurs, CEOs, and other leaders. The good news for you is that most of your competitors are among them, at least until they wake up to the need to build authority and read this book!

Let's start with the first fallacy—the belief that a company creates more lasting value through corporate branding than personality-based branding.

Smart businesspeople know that value isn't created through awareness—plenty of businesses have awareness all the way to the bottom of their industry.

Value also isn't created through pricing—price leverage is created as a result of value, not the other way around.

How is value created? Through a combination of problem solving and differentiation. Put simply, it is the speed with which you can show a potential customer/client that you provide a meaningful advantage over your competition and why that advantage means you are better suited to solve their problem.

That's where a corporate brand just doesn't deliver.

It is extremely difficult, time consuming, and expensive to differentiate one corporate brand from another. Not only do most business brands look and feel the same, but most small and medium-size companies have no business going head to head against much larger corporate brands in their industry that have been around for many decades longer and have marketing budgets a thousand times the size of theirs. They can simply outspend you into the ground.

Additionally, and perhaps most importantly, the speed to trust is dramatically slower with a corporate brand than it is with an individual brand of authority. It takes many more touchpoints and dollars to create affinity with a corporate brand compared to an authority brand—and the reason for that is simple. As the old saying goes, "People buy from people." Because we relate to a personality more easily than a business, the bond is easier to forge.

That's why creating an Authority Advantage for yourself is such a game changer. It allows you to punch above your weight class in terms of influence and visibility. Suppose you run a general financial advisory firm named Smith Wealth Management. How do you go head to head with, say, a powerhouse like Morgan Stanley?

Well, if you're a published author fresh off a CNBC appearance, where you established you're on a mission to help people, you're going to be more credible than a financial advisor handing out a Morgan Stanley business card, because that advisor is going to be perceived as more of a salesperson than an authority.

Here's what it comes down to. When your audience gets an email newsletter from noreply@yourcompany.com, they probably can't delete it quickly enough. But when they get an email from a mission-driven leader who has built affinity by providing value, they are expecting to learn something—because they see that person as an authority who can expand their thinking and their knowledge.

Dr. Andi Simon, the founder and CEO of Simon Associates Management Consultants, is a corporate anthropologist who helps executives see their companies with more observant eyes, achieve "aha!" moments, and discover new and profitable opportunities.

An author, speaker, and tenured professor, Andi realized that building her own personal credibility with the public was much more important than leading with her company brand, and we were happy to help her achieve that goal through our public relations services. Here, she explains her game plan:

> For Simon Associates Management Consultants, I deliberately blended my company's persona with my own. I was not interested in scaling the business. My goal was to create a successful management consulting firm founded on my expertise and experience as an anthropologist. People, I found very quickly, were buying trust in me. Whom I brought along was of less importance to them than I could be trusted to bring the right talent along to help them.
>
> *Trust* is a significant word for thought leaders. People listen to you and hope you have a solution for them. Whether working as an executive coach or with a team in a company, we must spend sufficient time together, so I become part of their story. We live our stories. Our minds want to feel safe with others. This means I must find ways to merge into their corporate culture or personal story.

As Andi makes clear, the personal connection is much more powerful than the company brand. We are dramatically quicker to trust individuals than we are corporations, and the quicker you can put that reality at the forefront of your strategy, the quicker you will win in this new environment.

THE PERSONAL CONNECTION IS MUCH MORE POWERFUL THAN THE COMPANY BRAND.

SHIFT 2: FROM CORPORATE MEDIA TO MICROMEDIA

The opportunity that smart content creation provides to leaders today is best understood by looking at the two most important contributing factors to its effectiveness: (1) trust, and (2) personalized value.

Let's talk about trust first.

As we mentioned in the lead-in to this book, the public is not only increasingly distrustful of corporate brands but also of corporate media, which it increasingly views as biased. This view used to be isolated to a select few media outlets that were known for their bias (some even embraced that bias), but as a result of media consolidation and increased polarization on all sides, we now watch, read, and listen to all media with a skeptical filter.

What we take in from the media may or may not be "fake news," but what is absolutely real in today's climate is our increased awareness and concern that it could be. While corporate media is losing our trust, the opposite is happening with what we call "micromedia"—individuals with the Authority Advantage who teach and provide value in a variety of forms, from books to YouTube videos to podcasts and beyond.

People put more trust in these types of micromedia than corporate media because they demonstrate expertise in a credible way.

For example—if we read a positive restaurant review in our local newspaper, we might wonder if the restaurant owner bought an ad in exchange for the glowing review, particularly when we see their ad show up a few pages later. When we hear a podcast hosted by a local food authority recommending the same restaurant, however, we perceive far less bias in their recommendation because the host seemingly has nothing to gain from praising the eatery. Its impact is similar to that of word-of-mouth recommendations. We trust what's being said because it's coming from a source we view as reliable.

Let's move on to the second contributing factor—personalized value, which has been perhaps the biggest accelerator of the growth of micromedia.

One of the challenges of building an audience as a large, generic media outlet is that you have to do your best to be all things to all people. As a result, when we listen to NPR, watch ESPN, or read the *New York Times*, we get a combination of content that matters to us as well as content that we simply aren't interested in. Because these outlets used to be the only game in town, we simply had to make the most of this fractional return on our time.

Until now.

Now we can get niche content at our fingertips that gives us a 100 percent return on our investment of time. Instead of listening to ESPN Radio, where we hear about lots of teams and lots of sports, we're listening to a podcast focused only on our team, such as Adam's Clemson Tigers or Rusty's Texas Longhorns. Instead of reading a general business publication, we're reading a newsletter on our specific niche. Instead of watching the national news, we can watch tailored news focused only on our industry niche via many different outlets.

How about you?

Do you find yourself "muting" general media that is giving you fractional value and instead giving your attention to micromedia that gives you exactly what you're looking for? More importantly—is your target audience doing the exact same thing?

Your audience increasingly wants to push major media out of the way to learn directly from you, something we hope is as empowering for you as it is exciting.

Are you giving them a chance to do that today?

SHIFT 3: FROM SELLING TO BUYING

Here's a question for you. Which is more important for a business: lead generation or sales?

Although there are loud voices on both sides of this debate, the practical answer for most businesses is simply yes, because most businesses have to climb both of these hills to grow.

The first hill of growth is generating leads for a business. This is difficult to do in any business climate but particularly so in today's environment of noise and disruption.

For the few businesses who are lucky enough to climb this first hill successfully and generate plenty of leads, they must now summit a second, bigger hill by convincing as many of those leads as possible to buy from them. The problem in this equation is the word *convince*, as most believe they have to resort to tactics like discounting or commoditizing their product or service to motivate action. This can result in them pushing prospects away or cannibalizing their own margins in the process.

THE HIGH GROUND OF AUTHORITY

The reason the concept of authority is so valuable for entrepreneurs and leaders is that you're not trying to drag uninterested leads up the second hill to sell them something, as most businesses attempt to do.

Instead, you begin on what business marketing guru Dan Kennedy calls "the high ground of authority." When you occupy this high ground, qualified leads are drawn to you because of your credibility and authenticity. They summit that hill on their own in a quest to learn. When they arrive at the top, they feel fortunate to be able to buy from you. You have put yourself in such a position of leverage that you are able to control which leads you allow to buy and at what price and under what terms.

This is counterintuitive for most entrepreneurs and leaders because it argues against something many of us were taught early on—that sales is the most important skill an entrepreneur can have.

But that's not true. People don't *want* to be sold something—they want to *buy* something. And the best way to get someone to seek out the opportunity to buy from you is to position yourself as the unquestionable authority in your space—someone they would be lucky to have a chance to do business with.

Patti Brennan, who we introduced you to in the last chapter, got past her initial

THE BEST WAY TO GET SOMEONE TO SEEK OUT THE OPPORTUNITY TO BUY FROM YOU IS TO POSITION YOURSELF AS THE UNQUESTIONABLE AUTHORITY IN YOUR SPACE.

doubts and decided to position herself as an authority with something to teach as she got more visible. In doing so, she found success and came out the wiser:

Authority isn't something where somebody can just give you a prize and say you are an authority. You have to earn it like anything. It's like trust—it doesn't just happen overnight; you have to earn it. And there are certain things that you can do to accelerate that process. It's how you conduct yourself at industry conferences, at meetings, with clients, even in the community.

Be seen as a leader, be it a thought leader, a giving leader, whatever your brand might be. And that's the foundation. To be honest, everybody has a bit of imposter syndrome. "Who says that my ideas are any better than anybody else's? Why would I be considered a thought leader?" You get those feelings of insecurity, like "I'm not nearly as good as so-and-so or so-and-so." To me, you still do it, because you learn along the way.

Patti's perspective here is so valuable because the imposter syndrome that she references is absolutely real in most leaders we interact with.

So, how do you get over that?

You worry less about yourself—and about those imaginary people you mistakenly believe might be looking at you as an imposter—and instead you focus on serving others with great content. That mindset shift creates the drive and motivation to start down this road of building authority because of the visualization of the impact you can make.

Over time, as you start to receive emails from those whose lives have been changed by your message, you become much easier to motivate, because the impact is real and apparent. Unfortunately, the imposter syndrome Patti referenced prevents many leaders from ever getting started and, as a result, from those emails ever being sent by those whose lives might have been changed.

Don't let that happen to you.

3

THE AUTHORITY MATRIX

BEFORE WE START building your Authority MAP, let's take a look at the framework we use to chart the impact of a leader in today's landscape.

From our experience working with thousands of leaders over the past twenty years, from Forbes 400 members to from-scratch multimillionaire entrepreneurs, we have learned to organize the reach and impact each leader makes according to what we call the Authority Matrix.

LEADERSHIP IMPACT

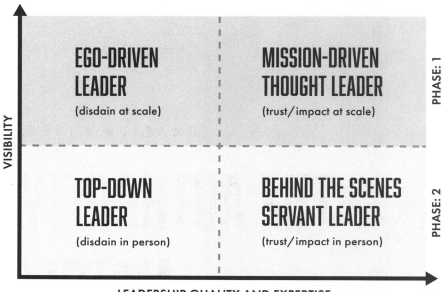

We believe all modern leaders can be associated with one of the four archetypes listed above. Their location on this matrix defines not only the scale of the impact that they make but also the trust they build (and with whom).

The x-axis across the bottom represents the quality of your leadership and expertise. This is what those who deal with you directly (your coworkers, clients, direct reports, vendors, strategic partners, family, and friends) see. This requires no level of visibility whatsoever beyond those who come in direct contact with you.

The y-axis represents the scale of your impact based on how visible you and your message are *beyond* those who deal with you directly. This could be accomplished through community engagement, public relations (PR), speaking, social media, events, books, or other forms of teaching at scale. Think of this as the reach of your message via your thought leadership platform or public-facing authority brand.

Just like there are bad behind-the-scenes leaders, there are plenty of people who build visibility the wrong way. In fact, when some of you picked up this book and saw a reference to personal branding or thought leadership, the Ego-Driven Leader may have been the first archetype that immediately came to your mind.

THERE ARE PLENTY OF PEOPLE WHO BUILD VISIBILITY THE WRONG WAY.

To be clear, the size of your following has nothing to do with whether you are in the left or right quadrant in terms of your impact; it just plots how high you are on the y-axis. Instead, what determines the quadrant you are in is the way you approach building visibility.

Are you doing it in an ego-driven, "Hey, look at me!" kind of way that is meant to make you look good? (Spoiler alert: it doesn't.) Or are you creating content and getting active as a way to serve others at scale (which we define as Mission-Driven Authority)?

Let's take a closer look at each of the four archetypes within the Authority Matrix.

ARCHETYPE 1: THE TOP-DOWN LEADER

Here's the problem with top-down leadership: if the leader doesn't see a problem coming, they will deny it exists.

The Top-Down Leader is the "boss" who's always right in his mind and expects others to agree with that assessment. It's a traditional and limited view of leadership that often excludes valuable input from others who might have crucial information to share. (Michael Scott, anyone?) This kind of leader risks alienating not only their own people but also potential clients and customers, because their egos often make them blind to their lack of communication skills.

If you fall into this category, let's redirect your attention toward leadership coaching before attempting to build your Authority Advantage so that you're in the best position to profit from it.

MENTALITY: "How can others serve me?"

REACH: Limited to those who come in direct contact with them.

KNOWN AS: A leader who often shoots themselves in the foot because of their ego.

ARCHETYPE 2: THE BEHIND-THE-SCENES SERVANT LEADER

In contrast to the Top-Down Leader, the Servant Leader is determined to put their head down to meet the needs of their people.

This archetype has been successful in their career by serving those around them. They take great pride in generating referrals, retaining team members, and building goodwill with those who come in direct contact with them.

Yet despite all the great things they are doing, they constantly hear their company is "the best-kept secret" in their industry. Their growth and impact are slowed by the lack of visibility at any kind of scale. Put simply, their impact is limited to those who are lucky enough to come in direct contact with them, such as a patient at their clinic, a client they directly engage with, or a member of their community. That limited exposure prevents them from reaching their full potential.

This archetype has the most to gain from building their Authority Advantage and the most to give to others as a result.

MENTALITY: Service and success. They put their heads down and overdeliver consistently for those who are lucky enough to discover them.

REACH: Limited to those who come in direct contact with them—either in person or by using their product or service—which stunts growth and keeps them on a hamster wheel.

KNOWN AS: The best-kept secret in their industry/space.

ARCHETYPE 3: THE EGO-DRIVEN LEADER

We've referred several times in this book to those who build their personal brand in a "Hey, look at me!" kind of way that grates on most people over time. This is what defines the Ego-Driven Leader.

This type of leader has plenty of visibility but is approaching it in the wrong way. By proclaiming constantly how great they are, they build a brand that reflects poorly on them and their business.

We can all think of someone like this, and they don't have to be sitting on the hood of a Lamborghini in an Instagram selfie to qualify for this category (although they certainly could be!).

Instead, this category is filled with people who overdo it with me-first content. "Look what I did! Look how smart I am. Look how much money I make!" are the messages that come across loud and clear with this archetype. A well-meaning leader may be trying to create an Authority Advantage in this manner, but it's the wrong approach.

If you recognize yourself in this category, the good news is that you can pivot if you follow the road map provided in this book to shift from showing wins to teaching others how to win.

MENTALITY: "Look how awesome/successful/smart I am!"

REACH: Largely limited to those who are related to them, who work for them, or who they have acquired by purchasing attention.

KNOWN AS: People who give personal branding a bad name via me-first content.

ARCHETYPE 4: THE MISSION-DRIVEN THOUGHT LEADER (THE AUTHORITY)

The Mission-Driven Thought Leader archetype is, we believe, the ideal one for a modern business leader. This type of leader has all the traits of a behind-the-scenes servant leader, with one hugely important additional advantage: they make a point of expanding the reach of the impact they make beyond those who are lucky enough to come in contact with them directly.

A Mission-Driven Thought Leader commands outsized influence in their space based on the value they provide, the size of their reach, and the third-party credibility they get from writing books, creating media, speaking, and authoring content. People trust them and follow their leadership.

As a result of the value of their public-facing brand, they generate independence, leverage, and impact at a level that gives them the ability to do exactly what they want to do with their life and career.

MENTALITY: View themselves as a Mission-Driven Authority with something to teach rather than an operator with something to sell.

REACH: Exponential.

KNOWN AS: The respected authority in their space.

If you aren't already a Mission-Driven Thought Leader, we're about to help you become one (and if you are one, we're going to help you get even bigger). In the next section of the book, we'll show you how to build your own Master Authority Plan (MAP).

PART TWO

BUILDING YOUR MASTER AUTHORITY PLAN (MAP)

HOW TO CREATE YOUR AUTHORITY ADVANTAGE

4

THE URGENCY OF BUILDING YOUR AUTHORITY BRAND

YOUR REPUTATION IS your lifeblood as a leader.

You know that. You know it defines the way others view you and often determines how likely (or unlikely) people are to want to work for or with you. Most leaders take great pride in working hard to develop a reputation as a servant leader with those around them. Our hope is that you fall into that category.

But have you ever thought about *how much* of the first impression others have of you is formed without any direct interaction with you? The answer might surprise you.

In today's media environment, the first place most people will interact with you and your brand won't be in person or even over the phone—it will be online, likely starting with search results and then continuing (if you're lucky) to your website and social media channels.

What's even more shocking to many leaders is that this is the case even when meeting someone in person! Think about it. What do you do before you head into that coffee shop to shake hands with the CEO you set a meeting with? You google their name from your car five minutes before the meeting, scrolling through the first page to get info about their background. Whatever you find in that quick scan forms your first impression, positive or negative, and it's an impression that will be very hard for that CEO to change in that meeting.

By the way, they've done the same to you! The real you is now in competition with the online you to live up to or overcome the first impression you made virtually.

And that virtual first impression is being created online whether you like it or not. Just because you "don't do social media" or you're "not interested in building a brand" doesn't mean that first impression isn't happening.

> **JUST BECAUSE YOU "DON'T DO SOCIAL MEDIA" OR YOU'RE "NOT INTERESTED IN BUILDING A BRAND" DOESN'T MEAN THAT FIRST IMPRESSION ISN'T HAPPENING.**

This is the point in the book where we want to grab you by the shoulders and look you in the eyes to make sure you're paying attention. If potential hires, customers, or partners are getting their first impression of you from their online searches far before they connect directly with you, don't you want to control that first impression and be intentional about that image so you can build trust instead of squandering that opportunity?

Of course you do—and that's the first step in building your Authority Advantage. This section of the book is going to take a deep dive into creating a personalized MAP that you will follow to create an authentic authority-driven image that differentiates you from others in your space.

WHAT IS BRANDING?

If we were to ask five hundred leaders for a definition of branding, we would likely get five hundred different answers.

Many people think branding is a logo, color scheme, or website while others would point to a mission statement or tagline.

Each of these things can contribute to creating a brand, but the definition of branding is much simpler:

> **BRANDING = CREATING AN IMAGE IN THE MINDS OF YOUR AUDIENCE**

Think about corporate brands like Delta Air Lines, Apple, the New York Yankees, the Olympics, or Uber—or individual brands like Elon Musk, Jamie Dimon, Kim Kardashian, or Gordon Ramsay.

When you come across those world-famous brand names, whether they relate to a corporation or an individual, an image or opinion likely comes to your mind. It could be positive or negative based on your experience with or opinion of those brands. The important point is that an image *does* come to your mind, which means they have successfully established a brand with you.

That is exceedingly valuable in today's noisy, competitive environment, but the reality is that having a visible brand has always been valuable for companies. The shift today is that individual brands have become an increasingly sought-after competitive advantage.

Let's look to Las Vegas and the job Caesars Entertainment has done leveraging one well-known celebrity's authority brand as an example.

GORDON RAMSAY AND THE VALUE OF AUTHORITY

We can learn a lot about branding from Las Vegas. The city itself has arguably the biggest brand of any in the United States, creating a distinct image in the minds of hundreds of millions around the world. Within Las Vegas, a second level of corporate brands exists underneath the city's umbrella, including publicly traded gaming empires like Caesars Entertainment, MGM, and Wynn along with hotel-specific brand names, including the Bellagio, Aria, Paris Las Vegas, Caesars Palace, and many others.

And while the lessons each can teach us could (and have) filled books, perhaps the most interesting thing that stands out when you walk down the strip is the strategic use of authority to attract attention and build trust.

Vegas is one of the best cities in the world at leveraging authority to drive traffic, from celebrities to performers to gambling personalities to chefs. And while there are many examples of the Authority Advantage in Sin City, one of our favorites is Gordon Ramsay, who has a deal with Caesars Entertainment to operate restaurants in the city under his name.

As of the writing of this book, they include the following:

- Gordon Ramsay Hell's Kitchen (Caesars Palace)

- Gordon Ramsay Pub & Grill (Caesars Palace)

- Gordon Ramsay Steak (Paris Las Vegas)

- Gordon Ramsay Burger (Planet Hollywood)

- Gordon Ramsay Fish & Chips (The LINQ Hotel)

Caesars also has Ramsay's name on restaurants at numerous other casino properties around the country, from Lake Tahoe to Atlantic City. In addition to licensing fees, Ramsay gets a cut of gross sales for each of the restaurants that amounts to a minimum of 5 percent with ramp-ups as sales go over $10 million, according to *Vital Vegas*.

Common wisdom might be that for that kind of payday, Caesars Entertainment would want Ramsay on site as much as possible—but that's actually the opposite of why he's so valuable to them. His contract requires the renowned chef to visit his Las Vegas locations only *once* each year and to stay for at least twenty-four consecutive hours.

Why do you think that is?

Caesars understands that the best and highest use for Ramsay isn't operating inside these businesses; it's building authority (trust and affinity!) through his books, TV shows, and other media ventures. He's most valuable to the company when his personality, perspective, and message are visible at scale—not behind the counter as an operator, although as we've seen on his various television shows, Ramsay is certainly capable of doing that well.

Put simply, he is worth far more for *who* he is than *what* he does.

His name leads every restaurant name. His picture appears on keycards for hotel guests checking in at many of Caesars' Vegas hotels. His image is used far and wide to generate interest in the properties themselves beyond just the restaurants.

While most authorities aren't going to have their name in lights up and down the Las Vegas strip (nor do we want that for most who read this book), we can learn a lot from Ramsay's use of media, books, and personality to differentiate himself in the very crowded and commoditized space of chefs.

The first lesson is that the knee-jerk reaction most leaders experience when they become more visible is the fear that clients will want more of their personal attention and that as a result this will prevent them from working *on* the business rather than in it.

We find the opposite is true for leaders who give themselves an Authority Advantage by building their personal brand. The more visible you are, the more you are perceived as a thought leader, and this causes customers to have a *lower* expectation that they will actually deal directly with you.

No one who walks into one of Gordon Ramsay's restaurants expects to see him behind the counter. Of course, that didn't happen for him overnight, but the more visible he became outside his eateries, the less patrons expected to see him in person.

The second lesson is one that is incredibly important for you to grasp—Ramsay has succeeded *not* by going with the pack but instead by being more of who he is—embracing his competitive spirit, showing a fiery four-letter-word personality, and committing to a style that endears him to viewers who trust him as a result.

Oh, and by the way—his Hell's Kitchen restaurant at Caesars Palace is well worth both the wait and the price.

Your space may not need a Gordon Ramsay–style personality (it probably doesn't!), but if you want to earn more for *who you are* rather than *what you do*—and make a bigger impact along the way—you'd be well served to channel your inner Ramsay as you show more of your own personality to build your brand.

Another great lesson from Ramsay is the power of authenticity to differentiate you from others in your space—something Mike Maddock learned early in his career. Over 25 percent of the Fortune

500 have trusted Mike to help them envision and create new sources of growth. We've been fortunate to work with Mike on publishing three of his best-selling books. In addition to being an author, Mike is a serial entrepreneur, global keynote speaker, and growth-strategy coach. He's also launched six successful companies, including Maddock Douglas. Here, Mike talks about how he uncovered the power of authenticity:

> I once spoke to the board of directors at Nationwide Insurance—and I wore a "Life Is Good" T-shirt under my suit jacket as well as jeans. The reason I wore jeans was because years ago, I woke up one day and realized I was dressing up to be on stage. I always wore jeans, but when I got on stage, I'd put slacks on. I was finally like, "What the hell is this? People are paying for authenticity, and I'm not being authentic in the way I dress." So, I just stopped. I said to myself, "You know what? I'm just going to wear jeans every day." Which, again, is what I wore when I spoke to Nationwide.
>
> A year and a half after that talk, someone said to the Nationwide CEO, "You remember Mike Maddock?"
>
> The CEO's reply? "Isn't that the guy that wore jeans in the boardroom?"
>
> There's something really powerful about being your authentic self … with the greatest authors and speakers, what you see is what you get; they're just themselves. So just be yourself, and let it show up on the page and on the stage. Brené Brown[2] always starts her talks with the same story where she was supposed to do a speech and her mind was spinning in circles about it. And she says to her husband, "I'm just going to tell

---

2   Authors' note: Brené Brown is an American research professor, known for her research on shame, vulnerability, and leadership.

them how I feel." And her husband goes, "No, don't do that. You're a researcher. Just stick with the data." And she says, "No, I just think I'm going to say how I feel." She broke down during her talk and exposed her fear, and she became immediately famous because she was authentic and vulnerable. I don't think that power can be understated. I think it's a really important part of what people are longing for in authorities.

We find many leaders who start to build visibility think they need to play some kind of role to be seen as an authority—but, as Mike states, that's the opposite of what really works.

In other words, don't water down your personality or try to copy someone else. What makes you authentic, trustworthy, and entertaining to your audience is you being more of yourself. We'll talk more about how to channel this uniqueness and authenticity as we unpack content strategy a bit further into the book.

While we know you recognize personal brands from Gordon Ramsay or Elon Musk, what about these names: Verne Harnish, Dr. Jamie Reynolds, Scott Manning, Sally Hogshead, or Jon Acuff?

Perhaps an image or opinion does come to your mind for these authorities if you have been introduced to them in the past, but our guess is probably not for all of them.

Each of these people is a stand-out authority in their space who has impacted tens of thousands of lives. If you didn't recognize their names, it means there isn't a brand yet in place with *you*. This is a starting point in fully understanding branding. The image you create in the minds of your audience always has an initial flashpoint, and frequently that flashpoint takes place without any direct interaction with you.

We just mentioned Verne Harnish's name. As the founder of the Young Entrepreneurs' Organization, now known as Entrepreneurs'

Organization (EO), and the Association of Collegiate Entrepreneurs, Verne is an authority whose impact has rippled across the globe, and all of us at Forbes Books feel fortunate to have published two of his books. His iconic 2014 bestseller *Scaling Up* serves as the foundation of his brand. Here's how he created his authority brand and connected it through his network, a network he himself built:

> My first step was putting together a partnership between MIT and *Inc.* magazine to launch an executive program for entrepreneurs back in 1991. A decade later, after having graduated over six hundred growth-minded entrepreneurs from the program, I curated what we had learned, and then I wrote/published *Mastering the Rockefeller Habits*. It was the second-most-important thing I did to start the authority journey—something I wish I had done a decade earlier. One innovation—we placed over a hundred testimonials in the front of the book, providing strong third-party endorsement for the tools/techniques allowed in the book. The third was referencing, in the book, my blog and encouraging readers to sign up. My weekly blog, which reaches just over a hundred thousand CEOs and CXOs, powers all our other activities—and my connection to the readers has led to the marketing of subsequent books.

Verne built his business by establishing a connection to his audience and serving them with a mission-driven mindset.

But before you can serve an audience at scale, you must create an image that causes them to trust you, so let's start with a smart audit of your brand, beginning with an understanding of the two phases of the branding process.

5

DEFINING YOUR BRAND

HOLLY WAS NOTORIOUSLY anti social media.

She wore it like a badge of honor, reminding her team, her family, and friends at every turn that she was too busy living her life to give others a play-by-play.

The CEO of a successful consultancy, she also took great pride in "not needing to do marketing" because her business was built entirely on the back of referrals from happy clients.

She was content with the growth curve for the business, which was respectable despite all opportunities coming inbound.

When we met with her, we can remember her telling us that her company's work speaks for itself and that she values one great referral more than "thousands of leads" from other sources.

Fair enough.

But what Holly wasn't considering was what happens once a happy client makes a referral. In most cases, the person referred doesn't immediately pick up the phone to request a proposal. Instead, they do some homework on Holly and her company to see if their friend who made the referral is an outlier in having a great experience with her. If the image created by Holly's online brand isn't congruent with the referral they received, it calls into question whether or not it's a fit.

In Holly's case, she had two things working against her that were leading to numerous referrals never taking action:

1. She shared a name with a well-known Olympian who dominated search results, which meant many who were referred to her by name weren't able to find her (we'll talk about how to solve this very common problem in this chapter).

2. For those who did find her LinkedIn profile, it looked like she lost the password back in 2014 based on how out of date it was. The website was also mailed in, creating questions for those referred to her on the quality of the business itself.

In other words, while Holly's business was generating plenty of referrals based on the quality of the work it did, she was only hearing from a small fraction of those who were actually referred to her based on neglecting (proudly!) the importance of her online brand.

Does this sound familiar? Have you taken pride in being a behind-the-scenes servant leader whose work speaks for itself?

If so, that head-in-the-sand approach to creating a brand is costing you and your team dearly. Just because you don't want to mess with building a brand doesn't mean others aren't getting a "brand image" of you online—it's just that you're not controlling what it is.

As a result, our expectation is that either no brand exists (because people can't find you!) or that it's not authentic to who you are (and the quality you provide).

If so, just like we worked with Holly to ramp the growth of her business by planting a more intentional flag for her as an authority, we want you to keep doing great work—but instead of letting it speak for itself, we want you to take a step forward so it can speak *louder*.

Let's take a deep dive on how to build an intentional, authentic brand as a leader.

> **JUST BECAUSE YOU DON'T WANT TO MESS WITH BUILDING A BRAND DOESN'T MEAN OTHERS AREN'T GETTING A "BRAND IMAGE" OF YOU ONLINE—IT'S JUST THAT YOU'RE NOT CONTROLLING WHAT IT IS.**

THE TWO PHASES OF BRANDING

As we mentioned in the previous chapter, branding is creating an image in the minds of your audience.

There are two distinct phases to doing that.

PHASE ONE = PREENGAGEMENT. This image is created before an individual has direct interaction with you, your company, or your message.

PHASE TWO = POSTENGAGEMENT. This image is created when the individual has had direct interaction with you as a customer, team member, prospect, partner, or even neighbor.

We're going to start with **PHASE TWO**, because it's the easier phase for leaders like Holly to identify with.

Postengagement begins when someone engages with you in some meaningful way, whether that's meeting with you for the first time, buying your product, reading your book, purchasing your service, listening to you give a speech, participating in your event, or joining your team as an employee.

The image you create in someone's mind in Phase Two is connected back to the answer to one very simple question: Did you overdeliver or underdeliver on their expectations?

This is true of any brand we do business with, be it a new restaurant down the street, a movie you took your family to see, a consultant you hired, or a book, like this one, that you chose to read. There was a "phase one" brand that got you in the door, but the ultimate image in your mind for each of those things is dependent on whether your expectations were missed, met, or—better yet—exceeded. Think about the brands you do business with. You are a repeat customer because the image they have created with you is a positive one based on the quality of their product, service, or content. They overdeliver.

For most businesses, Postengagement is driven by customer experience. If you are operationally competent and overdeliver on your promises, you likely have a solid Postengagement brand in place.

Evidence of a solid Postengagement brand includes customer referrals, positive customer reviews, team member retention, and growth.

Like Holly, many business owners and leaders are content to focus only on building a Postengagement brand. They put their heads down and drive toward one metric—pleasing the customer. As a result, they proudly proclaim that their business is built on the backs of referrals, often scoffing at brand building as something they "don't need to do." This kind of leader is trapped on the lower end of the y-axis on the Authority Matrix in terms of visibility despite being a great operator. As a result, this leader has put themselves in a risky position by relying only on Postengagement to drive growth and profitability.

The limiting factor of brands that rely primarily on Postengagement is that they have no direct control over lead flow. They have indirect control—by doing a good job for customers, they encourage them to refer new business, but they still have to sit back and hope their customer is at the right dinner party sitting next to the right person and that the right question comes up for that referral to happen. In short, a Postengagement business sits back and *hopes* the phone rings—they don't systematically pull a lever to create lead flow the way an Authority Advantage makes possible.

To be clear, we're not suggesting a successful brand or business can be created without consistently overdelivering for customers, team members, and stakeholders (in other words, doing Postengagement exceptionally well). But you already knew that—delighting customers is part of the table stakes for any business. In fact, if you're not doing Postengagement well (i.e., overdelivering for customers), then don't even consider building authority until you clean up your operations.

But we're going to assume you have a solid Postengagement brand in place with happy customers and a great team, and as such, the curve bender for your business's growth will be a systematic approach to creating your Authority Advantage.

That approach requires us to jump back to **PHASE ONE**—Preengagement branding.

As we discussed earlier in this section, the first flashpoint "image" that is created for you in the minds of your target audience will happen long before you ever interact directly with them.

Who is this true for?

- Potential customers (including those referred to you thanks to your Postengagement excellence)

- Potential strategic partners (including those referred to you)

- Journalists

- Meeting planners

- Influencers

- Potential employees

- Neighbors

- Potential in-laws

Here's the bottom line. In today's media environment, *your Preengagement brand is what Google says it is.*

What kind of impression are you making?

There are three must-haves when it comes to successful branding and omnipresence for those leaders who want to move up the y-axis and create an Authority Advantage in Preengagement:

1. Discoverability

2. Authority by association

3. Message clarity

Let's begin with discoverability, the most important of the three—which is all about making sure that when someone is looking for you, they can find you!

The first thing to consider before we concern ourselves with making a good impression is whether or not you are creating any impression at all.

Let's do a quick exercise, or what we call a brand audit. Open up your computer, open a private browsing tab (to remove location) and head over to www.Google.com. When you type in your name, what comes up?

We know from a recent HubSpot study that 75 percent of clicks on Google results happen in the first five results (above the fold, to use another newspaper expression), so let's focus on what links land in those first five spots.

If you own the results above the fold, ideally with a personal-brand website landing at number one, congratulations—you've aced the first metric of branding success in Preengagement: discoverability.

Ideally you should own all five results, but if you're not landing in the top five results in a search for your name, we have a major problem to solve before we worry about what kind of impression you are creating. We have to start with actually *creating* an impression.

Stats tell us it's unlikely someone will scroll very far, let alone pack a lunch and dig pages deep in Google, to search for you. That means we have a basic branding problem to solve—making you more discoverable.

If you don't show up at all, our first order of business is to consider why. Typically, it's one of two reasons:

1. You have an exceedingly common name that you share with hundreds of others, or you are unlucky enough to share an uncommon name with someone who is very visible, like an NFL player, a prominent politician, an actress, or an ax murderer from the seventies. Pray it's not the last one.

2. You haven't been active at all online and are missing out on the opportunity to own this first impression.

If the answer is the first one, as crazy as this may sound, we want you to consider changing your name.

Yes, you read that correctly.

While you may not have expected to change your name as a result of reading this book, this is a foundational starting point for many leaders who want to own search for those referred to them (or who come across their message).

Let's take David Meerman Scott, who wrote the foreword to this very book. His name is David Scott. Or was.

He wisely recognized early in his career that it was a name he would have a very hard time owning search for based on how common it was. He added in his middle name to ensure that when people referred to him or googled his name, he would be the person that would own that first impression instead of some other David Scott.

Similar to David, your name is a piece of digital real estate. If you have a common name like David Scott, you are currently sharing real estate with lots of other David Scotts. If you stick with that brand name, it's going to be very difficult to outrank all the others to own search on that name. This means that you're making it harder on yourself to generate results from marketing or referrals you receive because they will have a hard time finding you.

We realize that to some this sounds a little crazy. Maybe you haven't thought of your middle name or initial since grade school. It probably even sounds weird when you say it. Either way, it's about to come in very handy (and maybe even make that grandmother you got that middle name from even prouder of you!).

When you add a middle initial or middle name, you essentially walk across the street to a new piece of digital real estate that is completely empty. This allows you to plant your flag, lay claim to that land, and often immediately own search around your name.

The next step is to head to GoDaddy and see if your brand name is available as a URL (for example, AdamWitty.com or RustyShelton.com). If it's available, buy it today. While you're at it, buy the URLs for each of your kids and grandkids. This may seem silly at first blush, but you're essentially purchasing "lots" of virtual real estate that are valuable now and will only become more so in the future.

Your official brand name (middle initial or not) now goes on everything—on your business card, your speaker bio, your press mentions, your book cover, your Facebook page, your LinkedIn account, and everything else. It's "your" brand, and anywhere you are (whether being introduced for a keynote or shaking hands at a networking event), this is the brand you want out in front because it's the one you own and can build on.

We see a lot of leaders make the mistake of using inconsistent versions of their names. For some reason, this seems to be especially true for medical doctors and PhDs. On LinkedIn, they might have *Dr.* before their name while their website has *MD* after it. Oh, and their email signature might throw in a middle initial for good measure even though it's nowhere else to be found.

This kind of inconsistency is like scattering bricks on a bunch of different pieces of digital real estate. Not only do you confuse your audience, you also lose by not stacking all those bricks on *one* piece of real estate—so you can ensure you build the tallest tower of visibility when it comes to Google and other search engine algorithms.

We want you to be militant about consistency with your "brand" name. Once you decide what you're going with, we want the *exact same name* to appear everywhere.

You may not have picked up this book expecting to change your name by chapter 5, but getting clear and consistent with your brand name is a foundational step to building visibility and creating your Authority Advantage. Once you have a name you can own, the next step is to build an intentional brand.

In the next chapter, we'll explore the next two items on your online branding checklist: Authority by association and message clarity.

> BE MILITANT ABOUT CONSISTENCY. ONCE YOU DECIDE WHAT BRAND NAME YOU'RE GOING WITH ... THE EXACT SAME NAME SHOULD APPEAR EVERYWHERE.

6

BUILDING YOUR BRAND

THINK ABOUT YOUR INDUSTRY for a second. What is the most commoditized image that exists for someone who does what you do? In other words, if I'm referred to you and five others in your space, what is most likely to come up when I google everyone's name?

Here are a few examples of the most commoditized images we are likely to get across industries:

- **ATTORNEYS:** Usually a bio page on a law firm website with a formal headshot in front of a bookcase full of leather-bound legal books.

- **PHYSICIANS/DENTISTS/ORTHODONTISTS:** After weeding through Healthgrades, Vitals, and WebMD listings, if we happen to find your website, we're probably going to get a headshot of you in a white lab coat with a long list of facts, beginning with medical degrees, for your bio.

- **FINANCIAL ADVISORS:** We are most likely to get a bio page on a brokerage website or a LinkedIn profile with an attorney-style headshot in front of your desk or a bookshelf.

- **BUSINESS LEADERS:** For most business leaders we audit, we are lucky if we're able to find a LinkedIn profile that is sparsely updated with résumé-style information and a photo of a city skyline or beach sunset in the header picture area.

- **REAL ESTATE AGENTS:** Probably a photo of you from the waist up, leaning back with your arms crossed and a Sold sign behind you.

When you lead with the same commoditized images everyone else has, how do you expect to stand out or—better yet—build trust with a skeptical audience?

Let's consider financial advisors as an example.

Let's say I just sold my business. Now, I want to invest my proceeds in a smart way, and I receive five different referrals from friends. The first thing I'm going to do before I reach out to make an appointment with any of them is to kick the tires on those recommendations and make sure that whoever referred them isn't an outlier in terms of having had a great experience with the financial advisor.

I google their names, and in four out of the five cases, I land on bio pages within corporate websites from the likes of Edward Jones or Merrill Lynch. Perhaps I hit a LinkedIn profile that leads with a corporate logo or that ubiquitous sunset picture in the header and a normal headshot. Now, none of that is a negative—but neither is it exactly a positive.

The truth is, we're talking about the most commoditized images that could exist, and that puts me as a potential customer in a position of power. If I ever actually set an appointment with any of these advisors, I'm going to be grilling them about what they can offer me and what makes them different. It is a position in which *they have to sell to me* because no trust, other than the referral, was built ahead of time due to the lack of an authority brand. So, since all my candidates seem to have virtually the same qualifications, I'm going to make a decision based on convenience, price, and location, because that's how people shop for a commodity.

But what if one of those five referrals has created an Authority Advantage?

What if, when I googled one of the names, I landed on a personal-brand website built around this particular financial advisor. The first thing I see is the lead header image of them on stage giving a speech at their alma mater. Then I go on to note their recent media hits as well as an image of the cover of a book they wrote. Those images are balanced with content from them that focuses on their "why" and the mission behind what they provide for their clients. All that combines to both impress me and build trust—suddenly I'm feeling lucky to get in the room with this advisor. They're not available for four weeks? No problem—I'll wait. When I do arrive for that meeting, because they created trust before I walked in the door, I'm ready to learn from them, not grill them over fees and track record.

Do you see the difference?

How can you shift your image with your target audience from a commodity to a mission-driven thought leader your audience sees as an expert they can learn from?

Let's get intentional about doing just that.

AUTHORITY BY ASSOCIATION

After discoverability (which we explored in the last chapter), the next item to tackle is establishing *authority by association*, which accelerates the speed of trust.

Until your name is a brand that means something to a large audience (à la Gordon Ramsay), you differentiate yourself by associating yourself with brands that *do* mean something to your audience.

This is what is known as authority by association and is the single most important principle that exists when it comes to building trust with your target audience before you have a chance to interact directly with them.

This is such an effective tactic that one of the biggest brands in the world uses it to build trust and confidence with every single passenger boarding its planes.

We spend much of our time traveling, and it's been good to see air travel getting back to normal in this post-COVID-19 era. In fact, some of the things that used to annoy us about air travel are almost endearing this time around. Long lines at TSA checkpoints. Dirty looks between passengers elbowing their way into the boarding line. Heck, even fighting for an armrest in the middle seat feels nostalgic. Well, almost.

In addition to the trip down memory lane, here's another thing that caught our attention on a recent trip. Have you ever noticed the visual Delta Air Lines has just added to the side of the door as you walk onto the airplane? It's a case study in authority by association, as they feature logos from well-known media companies that have given awards to the airline in recent years.

Keep in mind, this is one of the most visible brands in the world, and they understand that it matters more what others say about them than what they say about themselves.

> No matter how successful you may be, don't make the mistake of discounting the importance of finding as many opportunities to associate your brand with existing brands that already have the respect and trust of your target audience.

You may not need to build a brand at thirty-five-thousand feet, but the Delta story provides a good reminder that no brand is flying so high that they can't benefit from authority by association.

Here's a test to determine how well you're doing with that concept at the moment. Pull out your professional bio, and read it carefully.

As you do so, note the following: How many established brands are you remarketing in that bio? Those brands could include media outlets, speakers you've shared the stage with, awards you've won, groups you're a part of, companies you've worked for, or more general categories like author, keynote speaker, or podcast guest.

Specific brands are far more powerful than general categories. For example, if someone tells you they are a keynote speaker, that's impressive but too general to meaningfully differentiate them from others. However, if they mention that they are a TED speaker or have shared the stage with Tony Robbins or Steve Forbes, their brand is along for the ride with the image that the TED, Tony Robbins, and

Steve Forbes brands have created in our minds, which is exponentially more powerful. Likewise, if someone tells you they are an author, that's very impressive—but not as impressive as someone telling you they are published by Forbes Books or Random House.

As you review your bio, look for ways to get more specific with your brands—you'll accelerate the speed of trust significantly with your reader.

VISUAL AUTHORITY BY ASSOCIATION

Although a text bio is incredibly important, in today's landscape most Preengagement brand images are created virtually. As a result, most people won't be willing to make it to your bio unless you can entice them with the right visual immediately upon landing on your website or LinkedIn profile.

We recently met with an accomplished speaker who was getting market resistance to raising his keynote speaking fee. He had spoken at TEDx along with many other top venues but was having to price himself far under the market. After a brief review of his marketing materials, we clearly saw that his problem wasn't his expertise or the quality of his speaking—his problem was the way the market perceived his authority.

Let's start with his website.

Like most speakers, the lead image on his home page was one of him on stage speaking, but the visual gave the viewer no indication of where he was speaking, the size of the audience, or the message itself. In showcasing this image, he was associating himself with a general brand (speaking) but wasn't giving his audience a more specific brand to take his authority to the next level.

A simple change in this visual—shifting from a generic speaking picture to a speaking picture on stage with the TEDx logo behind him and the sizable crowd in view—gives a dramatically different image in the mind of the site visitor. That visitor will be getting their first impression of this speaker, and that first impression will be markedly improved because the visitor will immediately link the speaker with TEDx. As a result, the meeting planner who is searching for a high-profile speaker is feeling fortunate he's only charging $20,000 for a keynote (which was twice what he was charging before)—all because he leveraged the value equation with authority by association.

Now, let's talk about your website.

When a visitor arrives on your website, what visuals are they met with? Is it a stock photo of a smiling couple? A picture of you behind a desk? Perhaps a headshot you just had taken? If so, your brand is stuck at the bottom of the authority mountain alongside most of your competitors who are doing next to nothing to build authority by association.

Orthodontists frequently rely on smiling teenagers for their header image. Many lawyers are fond of sitting behind desks holding pens. Financial advisors pose with their teams or have the exact same stock photo of grandparents walking on the beach with their stock photo grandkids. Don't join them in the quicksand of commoditized visuals.

Instead, the visitor to your website should be met with visuals that immediately establish authority by association.

We recommend the following one-two-three punch:

1. **HEADER IMAGE:** Ideally this is a picture of you on stage giving a speech with the logo of a recognizable brand behind you and a sizable audience in view. The site visitor has no idea who you are because it's their first impression of you, but they recognize that Forbes logo on the curtain behind you and are now wondering if they can afford your speaking fee or if you're even available for their conference dates.

2. **SPECIFIC LOGO BELT:** As we have discussed, nothing boosts your authority like specific brands you are associated with. Our top choice for most of you is remarketing media coverage from brand-name media outlets. We want those logos front and center on your website in addition to being showcased in the text in your bio. Right under your main header image, showcase four to eight media logos of outlets that have featured you in the past. Another way to attack this is to spotlight logos of recognizable companies you have worked with or awards you have won.

3. **BOOK COVER(S):** If you are a published author, you want to make sure a 3D image of the book cover is right underneath the specific logo (ideally with a best-seller burst, if applicable).

Here's an example of how authority by association can quickly expand your networking power.

Dr. Michelle Johnston is a management professor, executive coach, keynote speaker, and best-selling author of *The Seismic Shift in Leadership: How to Thrive in a New Era of Connection.* When she began her publishing journey, she discovered for herself the incredible power of authority by association.

> I got on LinkedIn and started posting, talking about the book and the leaders that I was interviewing and what I was learning, and I started to build a following. And what really was a game changer around the same time was when Marshall Goldsmith, who is the number one executive coach in the world, a *New York Times* best-selling author and the number one global thought leader, became my mentor.

> I didn't know much about social media back then, so I didn't realize that me posting a picture of me and Marshall

as my mentor and him agreeing to write the endorsement to my book would catapult me into his network. And all of a sudden, I had thousands and thousands of views on that post. And then he asked me to be a part of his elite organization called the 100 Coaches. So now, all of a sudden, I'm with other *New York Times* best-selling authors and other global thought leaders with their vast networks. It's just wild how this works.

MESSAGE CLARITY

The best authority brands walk a tightrope between visually establishing credibility while also advancing mission-driven thought leadership.

You want the visuals on your website, LinkedIn profile, Twitter account, and elsewhere to say what you don't want to say about yourself: media personality; stand-out thought leader; top-of-her-game, lucky-if-I-can-do-business-with-her leader. At the same time, the text should establish personality and clearly communicate the "why" behind your work. This is essential to achieving the third step in the Preengagement phase, *message clarity*. You don't want people guessing what you're trying to say. You want to say it clearly and in the most impactful way.

As you grow your visibility as an authority, more and more people are going to land on your website seeking to learn from you instead

SAY IT CLEARLY AND IN THE MOST IMPACTFUL WAY.

of immediately being ready to buy. We want the visuals within your website to give them a reason to pay attention to your message. Then we want the message you advance to clearly communicate why you are the absolute best fit for your target audience. That happens when your message is equal parts personality and purpose—we'll be covering more about that important balance as we get into the next section of the book.

Creating your Authority Advantage isn't all about creating the right image—but you cannot build meaningful momentum unless you do.

Without that visible brand in place, you may generate significant attention via content marketing, public relations, speaking, events, or referral marketing. But you're unlikely to generate audience growth and lead flow because people looking for you online don't get a Preengagement impression that is congruent with the quality you will provide in Postengagement.

Here's how Verne Harnish followed through on establishing message clarity in a deliberate and successful manner:

> The key to marketing is owning a word or two in the minds of enough people to scale a business. The title of the book *Scaling Up* was chosen to cement our ownership of these two words. We took the additional step to change the name of our coaching and consulting firm to Scaling Up and launched a media site called www.scaleups.com to own the related term *scale ups*.
>
> We like to think the book is our "first impression," and then the website serves as a way to guide people in getting the support they need in implementing our tools/techniques. The book serves as a complete "business card"—and all our efforts are to market the book, with just over 500,000 of *Scaling Up* and 850,000 of all four books in the market—print, audio, and e-book.
>
> We include 500 books with every speaking gig, which provides both exposure from stage and something they can

take with them afterward to read if they found the presentation useful. In addition, our 200+ coaching partners host regular one-day workshops that further introduce potential clients to the power of our approach to scaling without all the drama normally associated with growing a firm.

Make no mistake—there is a high cost to ignoring any phase of branding. If you ignore Preengagement like Holly previously did, you remove the potential to create impact, value, and trust at scale. If you ignore Postengagement, you have a ticking time bomb on your hands in terms of negativity because you aren't overdelivering for those who work with you.

In our experience, most entrepreneurs intuitively understand the importance of Postengagement (or they wouldn't have a legitimate business) but ignore or stumble through Phase One (Preengagement) of branding, which is why creating your Authority Advantage is such an accelerant to growth and gives you a distinct edge over the competition.

The good news?

The most immediate impact you will see from building an authority brand will be among those who already know and love you. They will be much more likely to refer you when they know it's going to make them look good as a result.

Dr. Andi Simon, who we introduced you to in chapter 2, found this out for herself as she carefully created her authority brand from the ground up. The results spoke for themselves:

> When I launched my business in 2002, twenty years ago, I was coming off almost twenty years of being a corporate executive in financial services firms and healthcare institutions. I met with my PR firm, and we talked about who

I was and what I did for my future clients, as well as my academic background as a cultural anthropologist. It was his idea to frame myself as a corporate anthropologist specializing in helping organizations change.

Since that day, that is the sentence that has been my brand, as well as my purpose and my passion. Most people hate change. The brain fights it. Even when their business is struggling, they tend to resist the new and fight the unfamiliar. My job was to show them how to embrace change, see, feel, and think in new ways, and sustain their growth, as a person and a business, through changing times.

To some degree, I applied similar methods to launch and grow my business in a category—corporate anthropology—that was unknown at the time and unclear to most potential users. I found that I had to do several things rather quickly and consistently to grow my reputation and personal brand. These included the following:

1. Crafting a story that clearly explained what they needed and how I could help them solve their pain or problem. Since they were less concerned with how I would do it, I could slip past the endless questions about what it was an anthropologist did. Instead, I could get to how we would work together to dissect the hurdles and their limits to growth and find new pathways. These were often all around them, if only they could see the possibilities. I also took them out exploring with me as if they were anthropologists searching for new ways to find clients, solve problems, and sustain their growth. They, in turn, would refer me to their colleagues who were stuck or stalled.

2. Using written materials, which were essential to help others better understand what I did and how I did it. I loved content marketing and began to build my website with all forms of material—videos, webinars, white papers, blogs, and podcasts. For me to establish and sustain myself, I had to be myself. But I also had to help clients understand what they were buying and what they would do with me to address their challenges. It was very much a "we" strategy. I could not achieve success unless my clients worked with me to deconstruct their business and go exploring to see other ideas and options all around them.

3. Conducting workshops, which was a very useful way to engage with prospective clients, show them how to see through a fresh lens, and sell me as a solution for their business challenges. It worked, and I had a steady stream of clients from these workshops.

By defining her brand, backing it up through strong content marketing, and extending that brand into her professional interactions, Andi not only established what she was all about—she also generated a steady stream of referrals.

In the next chapter, we're going to show you how to empower more referrals as a result of building your Authority Advantage, just as Andi did.

7

SHOWCASING YOUR BRAND

RUSTY HAD NEVER been to Detroit but was excited to be invited to speak at an event there to be hosted by Dr. Jamie Reynolds (www.ask-drreynolds.com), a longtime member of the Advantage Media family. Dr. Reynolds leads Spillane & Reynolds (www.myamazingsmile.com), one of the fastest-growing orthodontic practices in the Midwest. He is a true example of a mission-driven authority in his space.

The event was held for dentists at the historic Shinola Hotel in downtown Detroit as a way to thank them for referring patients to Dr. Reynolds's practice and being a part of the community. On their way to the venue on the morning of the speech, Dr. Reynolds stopped by their newest location in the growing suburbs of the city to show Rusty the new office. The vibe was fantastic—incredible attention to detail on the branding and plenty of things for kids to do while they are waiting. But what caught Rusty's eye was something that seemed out of place in a normal orthodontic practice: a giant gold gong.

The obvious question came next: "What's the deal with this gold gong?"

Dr. Reynolds laughed and explained that like most orthodontic practices (and most businesses), they rely heavily on referrals from dentists and happy patients. The starting point for them in generating referrals is overdelivering in Postengagement by being intensely focused on both the patient experience and team-member happiness.

But Dr. Reynolds knew that creating happy patients alone isn't enough for the kind of growth he wanted. Instead, he wanted to find a way to intentionally empower them to talk about their experience with his practice in a fun way.

That's where the gong comes in.

We should probably explain that the referral marketing process at most orthodontic practices goes something like this: The patient finishes the last appointment and walks up to the counter with her parents so they can pay the final bill. During the interaction, the front desk clerk, who has been coached to let the patients know that referrals are the lifeblood of the practice, asks, "Do you know any other parents looking for a great practice to put braces on their child?" as she pushes a couple of referral brochures toward the customer.

Super awkward for everyone involved in that interaction.

Instead of following that transactional (and ineffective) approach to referrals, Dr. Reynolds focused on empowering patients and their families to talk about the "wow" experience they had. They have worked to create a vibe that feels like the patient is winning by intentionally creating a "referral moment," and this brings us back to the gong.

When a patient gets their braces off, everyone in the office stops what they're doing—from the front desk all the way to back-office staff—and gathers around the gong in the main practice room. Other patients turn and watch as well as the teen, with their beautiful new smile, bangs the gong as everyone cheers. Not only is that an authentic, super-memorable moment for that teen, but the mom or dad of the teen who just banged the gong can't get that video on Instagram and Facebook quick enough. And when she posts it, she's likely not only talking about Samantha's great new smile—she's also talking about how awesome Spillane & Reynolds have been along the way. Think about how that compares to the typical afterthought request for referrals and the awkward sales brochure handoff.

This kind of "referral moment" creates a true win-win scenario because the content is something that the referring party actually is excited to share, and it empowers them to talk about one of the best Postengagement orthodontic experiences in the entire country—which only happens at Spillane & Reynolds.

REFERRAL MARKETING: HOW TO CREATE A BRAND OTHERS WANT TO ASSOCIATE WITH

The Word-of-Mouth Marketing Association reports that every day in the United States there are approximately 2.4 billion brand-related conversations. How many of those 2.4 billion conversations revolve around your brand, and what can you do to ensure that you spark more positive ones in the future? We're going to explore both of those questions in this section of the book.

Few words are better to hear early in a conversation with a new lead than "I was referred by ..."

That line changes the sales dynamic immediately because of the level of trust that is already in place based on their friend vouching for your brand. This allows you to immediately shift from convincing them why you're the best person to solve their problem to actually solving it.

In addition to being the best source of "fast-track" leads, referrals provide a shot of validation to leaders that customers and partners are impressed enough with the product or service to talk about it to others.

Although there are many reasons to love referrals, far too many leaders and business owners get trapped into an overreliance on them to bend their growth curve. When we ask leaders how they drive leads for their business, many will puff out their chests a bit and say something along the lines of "We're entirely built on referrals."

That kind of response tells us two things about a business:

1. They have a great operational business that is overdelivering for customers (the foundation of every successful business).

2. They are likely growing at a slow rate, particularly if they are sitting back and waiting for customers to refer rather than intentionally driving those referrals.

So, while they're proud as a peacock based on the first item, the second item is secretly keeping them awake at night because they have no direct control over their lead flow. If you rely on referrals for a significant percentage of your lead flow, and you aren't doing anything to intentionally drive them, like Dr. Reynolds, you're beholden to both the willingness and happenstance opportunity your customers have to refer you.

Again, we're not saying having a business reliant on Postengagement isn't a positive. It's usually a sign of a very good operational business. If customer experience wasn't good, those referrals wouldn't be flowing in, right?

The problem is that when you rely entirely on other people to drive lead flow, you put yourself in a risky position, because you have limited direct impact on lead generation. Sure, you have plenty of indirect influence on driving referrals by doing a great job for customers, but true referral marketing is a shift from sitting back and passively waiting for referrals to actively driving them.

Put simply, you are sitting around waiting for the phone to ring. This is a helpless feeling for an entrepreneur or leader, but it is the reality for many—even when they do great work (like the behind-the-scenes servant leader archetype)!

We'll leave doing the great work to you, but let's explore the art of referral marketing and why it is such an important component of your Authority Advantage.

WHY DO PEOPLE REFER?

There are thousands of country clubs in the United States, and many of them battle the exact same challenge: driving more memberships. These clubs spend millions of dollars each year on branding, advertising, direct mail, social media, open houses, young family programs, camps, and other promotional campaigns meant to drum up interest with potential members.

However, it's often a very tough sell, as country clubs are competing with public golf courses, neighborhood pools, restaurants, and other pulls on expendable income. The increased competition is one of the reasons this industry is on the decline.

Although many country clubs recognize that referrals from existing members are the quickest way to achieve new-member goals, very few of them understand how to properly motivate those members to actively and excitedly refer friends.

There are two reasons we refer others to products or services:

1. We believe the product or service is something that will delight that person, and we're willing to stand behind it.

2. Our ability to refer others to that product or service is something that makes us look good.

Think about it: typically, the referral you are most proud to make is the one where there is an air of scarcity or authority involved.

- "The new five-star restaurant downtown is booked a month out, but I know the owner. I'll work on getting you and your in-laws a table."

- "Sorry to hear about your injury. Have you seen Dr. Mahr yet? He's the best shoulder surgeon in the South, and he's typically booked out eight months ... but let me reach out to him and see if he'll make an exception for you."

- "My executive coach only takes on eight clients a year, and he hasn't had an opening for the past three years, but I'll reach out to him and see about getting you on the waiting list."

What's consistent about each of these referrals above? The person making the referral is excitedly doing so because it makes them look good by having access to a velvet-rope referral. Everyone else is standing in a line around the block, but you're being told, "Here, come to the VIP line, and let me personally get you to the front."

The person who makes this kind of referral enjoys what we call the "authority halo." They are suddenly seen as a more impressive individual because they can provide access to these kinds of in-demand authorities. In the end, good authority-driven referral marketing creates a win-win-win for you, your customer, and your new lead in the following ways:

- You generate leads more consistently and with the expectation of an up-market experience based on exclusivity.

- Your customer actively and excitedly refers you as much as they can because of the authority halo it delivers to them in the minds of others.

- Your new lead gets the benefit of having a chance to consume your product or service and be better off as a result.

Let's go back to the country club conundrum for a second. The quickest way for a country club to begin a race to the bottom is to run a campaign built around discounts and availability.

This type of campaign does three things that work against its goals of adding new members:

1. It makes current members question the value of their membership because of the "on the cheap" approach (hint— current members will not be asking about the referral program despite the invite at the bottom).

2. It turns a membership into a price-based commodity for potential members, which dilutes the attraction.

3. It gives off a vibe of desperation.

A much better approach would have been to announce—with the largest possible exposure—that the club is no longer taking on new members. This kind of announcement creates excitement, intrigue, and interest among existing members and the community because a velvet rope has now been placed around the property.

All of a sudden, the country club is viewed differently by those both inside and outside the ropes. Members who weeks earlier were complaining about the lukewarm water cooler on the number thirteen green or the coloration on the number seven green are walking a bit taller and looking for as many opportunities as possible to wear anything with that country club logo on it. Conversations at weddings and other events hosted there feature comments like this: "Did you know this place isn't taking on new members anymore? I'm kicking myself—I had a chance to join a few years back, and I should have jumped on it."

That country club now has a brand that is long on authority, which shifts the dynamic for all involved. Instead of having to ask members to refer friends or creating dynamic referral campaigns, members now beg to get their friends to the top of the waiting list.

> ### HERE'S THE BOTTOM LINE: NOTHING MAKES US WANT TO REFER LIKE THE ABILITY TO UNHOOK A VELVET ROPE AND WALK OUR FRIENDS TO THE FRONT OF THE LINE.

Here's the bottom line: *nothing makes us want to refer like the ability to unhook a velvet rope and walk our friends to the front of the line.* It's counterintuitive, but the best way to drive referrals to your business is to channel your inner Augusta National and go heavy on both authority and exclusivity. As a result, you will enjoy the bright shine of the authority halo.

DOES YOUR BRAND ENCOURAGE OTHERS TO REFER?

Many leaders are frustrated because they believe they are the absolute best in class in their given industry—but other competitors seem to generate more referrals.

It's important to understand that being best in class is just the starting point to driving referrals, whether you are a speaker, financial advisor, or consultant.

Your Phase One image (Preengagement) must be congruent with the quality you provide in Phase Two (Postengagement). One of the most immediate impacts of building your Authority Advantage is how much it empowers those who already know and love you to talk about their experience working with you more frequently.

Why does this happen? Just like the country club that becomes more exclusive, when you write the book on the topic or have a brand that validates their decision to work with you, it makes them look good for being able to make that connection.

WHO IS REFERRING YOU, AND HOW CAN YOU EMPOWER THEM?

When your authority brand is established, you'll want to then empower more referrals intentionally.

Do you have clarity on who is referring to you? Many leaders make the mistake of focusing their referral marketing efforts only on customers, which limits the reach of such campaigns.

The reality is that most businesses have three key categories of referral drivers:

- Customers

- Referral partners/strategic partners (typically other businesses)

- Influencers (typically individuals who benefit from referring you)

If you don't currently have a way to track the sources of your referrals, you must put such a system in place. Depending on volume, you may be able to start with something as simple as an Excel document with three tabs (one for each of the categories above). Use these tabs to organize both existing referral bases and ones you want to target.

Once you have a clear view of who is referring to you right now, the next step is to think about how you can better empower them to refer to you more often in the future. One of the most effective ways to empower each of the groups above is to involve them in your content-marketing efforts.

In our experience, the best way to give people a reason to talk to others about their experience with you is to create a moment where they are *involved* in the experience, á la Dr. Reynolds.

But the good news is, you don't need a gold gong in a well-designed office location to do that. Instead, as you create your Authority Advantage, you can use your book, content strategy, and other efforts to build intentional relationships with both current network members and those you want to get to know. We're going to show you how to do that in this next section.

BUILDING YOUR CONTENT STRATEGY

We spent a lot of time earlier in this book on the importance of earning the right to teach and educate your audience by building trust. This is why your brand is so important. But once you build trust, your audience is leaning in to learn from you, and this is where your content strategy comes in.

Nothing is more important to building an audience, driving revenue, and making an impact than the ability to create high-quality content. Yet few thought leaders understand how to do it.

Rather than exploring what kind of content their audience is seeking, most are more concerned with where they should be posting that content. *Should I be on Twitter? Does it make sense to start a podcast now that everyone seems to have one? Is YouTube still the most important for SEO? My kid says TikTok is the new thing—is that right?*

These are not bad questions; it's just that the "where" of content is far less important than the "what" of content. In other words, what kind of content is your audience looking for? Once we know that, the distribution of that content is the easier part. After all, nowadays most content is omnichannel and is distributed in one form or another across multiple platforms.

Videos used to be for YouTube. Photos used to be for Instagram. Text used to be for blogs. It's all for everything today, with an emphasis on "native" content to improve the organic reach of your content and brand on each various platform.

The platforms where we post content will keep changing, and new ones will continue to come onto the scene. The thing that will remain the same is the need to entertain and inform with your content, no matter the format.

CONTENT IS KING

When it comes to building thought leadership, the quote "content is king" is probably shared more than any other one. It originated in a famed essay Microsoft cofounder Bill Gates wrote and published on the Microsoft website all the way back in 1996 where he describes the future of the internet as a marketplace for content.

Here's an excerpt from that essay:[3]

Content is where I expect much of the real money will be made on the internet, just as it was in broadcasting.

---

3   Bill Gates, "Content Is King," Microsoft.com, January 26, 2001, http://www.microsoft.com/billgates/columns/1996essay/essay960103.asp. Internet archive, http://web.archive.org/web/20010126005200/http://www.microsoft.com/billgates/columns/1996essay/essay960103.asp.

The television revolution that began half a century ago spawned a number of industries, including the manufacturing of TV sets, but the long-term winners were those who used the medium to deliver information and entertainment.

When it comes to an interactive network such as the internet, the definition of *content* becomes very wide. For example, computer software is a form of content—an extremely important one—and the one that for Microsoft will remain by far the most important. But the broad opportunities for most companies involve supplying information or entertainment. No company is too small to participate.

One of the exciting things about the internet is that anyone with a PC and a modem can publish whatever content they can create. In a sense, the internet is the multimedia equivalent of the photocopier. It allows material to be duplicated at low cost, no matter the size of the audience. The internet also allows information to be distributed worldwide at basically zero marginal cost to the publisher. Opportunities are remarkable, and many companies are laying plans to create content for the internet.

If people are to be expected to put up with turning on a computer to read a screen, they must be rewarded with deep and extremely up-to-date information that they can explore at will. They need to have audio, and possibly video. They need an opportunity for personal involvement that goes far beyond that offered through the letters-to-the-editor pages of print magazines.

Gates was remarkably on target with this essay he wrote more than twenty-five years ago. He saw the internet as a frontier that would democratize ideas and give those willing to create content a chance to reach a global audience without spending a fortune.

While many leaders view the need to create content as a chore or distraction, the reality is that those who do this well give themselves significant leverage to own the connection with their audience and build the kind of trust and affinity they have been gifted at doing in person at scale.

Understanding the importance of content to your success moving forward, we want to give you a specific road map that focuses your time on the best and highest use for your organization and objectives.

But first, let's take a big picture look at the current media environment.

THE AGE OF MICROMEDIA

Here's a crucial point about today's media environment: *Every individual and brand is a media outlet, whether they know it or not.*

Some are influencing a few hundred people through a Facebook page or LinkedIn profile. Others, those who have embraced the micromedia mindset, own subscription bases larger than their local newspaper.

> EVERY INDIVIDUAL AND BRAND IS A MEDIA OUTLET, WHETHER THEY KNOW IT OR NOT.

Joe Rogan is an interesting case study. Since its launch in 2009, *The Joe Rogan Experience* has become one of the most popular podcasts in America, downloaded nearly two hundred million times per month and bringing in $30 million annually. In 2019, Rogan was the highest-paid podcaster in the world and cut a very large deal ($100 million, to be exact) to move his content to Spotify as an anchor for their ambitious podcast network.

Like most top content creators, Rogan's approach is full of personality and mixes his own perspectives (complete with plenty of COVID-19 controversy) with carefully curated interviews from some of the world's most notable celebrities. But he didn't get there overnight. He started with a small audience and recognized that consistency would be a key component of success. He's now been doing it for more than a decade and, like many who build a large audience, has reached the point where he can walk away from everything else he doesn't want to do.

We don't want you to be Joe Rogan (unless you want to be—you can start by shaving your head ...), as most of you benefit most from building a targeted audience in your niche. But we do want you to use a smart content-marketing strategy and a willingness to show your personality to create the exact thing Rogan did: leverage.

YOUR CONTENT STRATEGY IS YOUR OWN PERSONAL NEWSPAPER

The best way to think of your content-marketing strategy is like your own personal newspaper (remember those?). Once you begin to view it in that context, you can avoid the kinds of mistakes that might doom a newspaper.

The most common mistakes we see are these:

- **SPORADIC DELIVERY:** Would you subscribe to a newspaper when you have no idea when it's being delivered?

- **AD HEAVY:** Many people oversaturate their newspaper/ content strategy with promotional "sales" posts that alienate their audience and often send them running for the exits in your stadium. Most people are smart enough to avoid breaking this cardinal rule, but it's a temptation that must be consistently resisted.

- **OP-EDS ONLY:** By far the most common mistake we see from experts is filling their newspaper with op-ed content—

meaning all the content is essentially their own perspective. This kind of content monologue works well if you're already a household name and your audience is full of people who know to pay attention to your expertise—again, think of Joe Rogan. However, this kind of me-first approach to content marketing is a slow grind in terms of growth. It is also exhausting because you have to create everything.

With these pitfalls in mind, how should you approach your content-marketing strategy? We'll tell you in the next chapter.

CHAPTER EIGHT:

THE THREE CATEGORIES OF CONTENT TO CREATE AN AUTHORITY ADVANTAGE

MOST LEADERS WE speak with intuitively know that they should be creating content, but they are often paralyzed by a lack of conviction on what content their audience is looking for.

Regardless of the category of media—earned, rented, or owned (we will dive deeper on these terms in the next section of this book)—and regardless of the format of the content—text, visual, audio, or video—we recommend you break your content evenly into three broad categories:

- You-Driven content
- News-Driven content
- Relationship-Driven content

Let's kick things off with the one that you are probably most familiar with—You-Driven content.

YOU-DRIVEN CONTENT

Most would-be thought leaders move forward with a content-marketing strategy filled overwhelmingly with this category of content.

In short, this is your stuff.

It connects back to your experiences, your personal journey, your perspective, your intellectual property, and your own resources. This kind of content is in great demand once you have a large audience in place but often equates to slow going when you're building that audience, because those who don't yet know you may struggle to understand why they should pay attention. As such, we want to limit this category to roughly one-third of the content you publish.

Ironically, one of our favorite success stories with this category of content is someone who used it for the bulk of his content.

Mike Travis heads up Travis & Company, a well-regarded boutique executive recruiting company based in Boston that focuses on the pharma/healthcare space. He called us several years ago wanting help with a brand refresh that included building a new website and updating his logo.

When we first spoke to him, we asked whether or not he had considered starting a blog. He said he'd thought about it but decided not to, based on two reasons.

The first reason was that his business was largely based on word-of-mouth referrals, and he was skeptical that a blog would benefit him since he was relying on people who already knew him.

The second reason was, he believed that his audience, C-level executives, didn't have time to consume longer-form content online. We agreed with him that most C-level execs wouldn't be habitual readers of the blog. But knowing the impact a good blog can have on discoverability (SEO, or search engine optimization), we encouraged Mike to start a blog as a way to grow his visibility with people who didn't yet know him but were looking for resources in the space. We believed this would diversify his lead flow beyond referrals (which are wonderful but outside his direct control).

Mike agreed to blog once a week for a year and then look back to see if we had achieved his goal of generating lead flow from the website outside his referral network. He focused his blog posts primarily on You-Driven content, educating readers on the nuances of executive recruiting, talent management, and the importance of the right kind of leadership in the rapidly changing pharma/healthcare space.

We checked in with him after eight months of blogging, and he gave us this update: "Traffic to my website is way up, and I've actually been enjoying blogging. But I haven't gotten a single lead from it yet."

Candidly, even though it takes time to get traction with the right content strategy, we were a bit surprised that his blogging hadn't generated lead flow. We encouraged him to continue through the year as planned because of the reality of You-Driven content: it is similar to laying bricks in a foundation for a house—one or two bricks don't do much, but the more you stack on each other, the more exponential the impact gets, particularly over time.

When we checked back in with Mike after the twelfth month, he had better news. His You-Driven content had generated several new leads that translated into three new clients. This delivered a six-figure ROI on his investment in addition to future lead flow from those posts.

One interesting lesson for Mike was that it wasn't always the C-level executive who found him via a blog post. Many times it was their assistant or team member who had been tasked with putting together a list of options on the recruiting side. When they searched for a top executive recruiter in the pharma/healthcare space, Mike's widened net caught those queries thanks to his diligent blogging.

It didn't happen overnight, and you shouldn't expect it to, but Mike's consistency and sophistication in terms of understanding his client base (and what kind of content they are looking for) delivered a major return on investment for his business.

WHAT ARE THE MOST COMMON TYPES OF YOU-DRIVEN CONTENT?

Although this category sounds pretty clear cut, there are actually a lot of different types of You-Driven content that you can create.

Evergreen Content

The most popular type of You-Driven content is evergreen content. This is content that is as valuable today as it's going to be years from now. This includes angles like "Four Questions HR Directors Should Ask before Hiring," "Three Ways Leaders Can Listen Better," and other more general approaches to your content strategy.

The best way to create evergreen content is to do exactly what Mike did and work backward from what you think your target audience is searching for on Google. But don't guess what your audience wants to read when coming up with content. Instead, work backward. Determine what your target audience is looking for online. What problem are they trying to solve? What questions do they want answered? What vexes them? Then, use your expertise and insight to answer their questions and furnish them with useful information. This kind of content generally focuses on broad topics or concepts pertinent to your industry and exists to capture those search results and pull in potential customers.

You can use Google's free tool at www.Trends.Google.com to see exactly which queries are getting searched and then create content around those queries in your space to start to widen your net to catch those inquiries.

Experience Shares

Both of us are members of EO. Adam is also in YPO (formerly known as Young Presidents' Organization). One of the seminal components of EO Forum is the willingness of members to share experiences. In EO, there is a strict code of confidentiality and an expectation that members of the Forum will "go 5 percent" with their updates, which means sharing the top 5 percent and bottom 5 percent of what's going on in their lives. One of the many reasons EO members develop such an immediate atmosphere of trust is the willingness to be vulnerable. This serves as an accelerant to trust in a way that almost nothing else can.

In this spirit, we want you to channel your inner Brené Brown (a thought leader whose brand is vulnerability and leadership) when you create You-Driven content. Be willing to peel back the curtain on the experiences, lessons, and challenges you have dealt with in your journey as a leader. And be honest about your emotional journey as well.

One of the best ways to both credential and endear yourself to an audience is your willingness to self-deprecate—and that tactic is a great way to approach this category of content. One of the best examples of this comes from Shawn Achor's famous TEDx Talk, "The Happy Secret to Better Work." It has been viewed more than twenty-four million times and is among the top twenty-five most-watched TED videos of all time. Although this is a speech, it provides a great lesson on how to balance building trust while bonding with the audience.

Achor opens the talk with a funny story about his sister and then transitions to the ever-important "evidence of expertise" component of the talk (in other words, why the audience should listen to you on this topic).

He wants the audience to know two things: 1) he went to Harvard, and 2) he's a data scientist. If he just comes out and tells the audience those two facts, they are going to be turned off by what might be perceived as arrogance. So, instead he makes fun of people who went to Harvard and also pokes fun at data scientists. As the audience is howling, they now know two things about Achor: 1) he went to Harvard, and 2) he is a data scientist. He has credentialed himself in an endearing way.

The best way to teach your audience a lesson is to start with the biggest "flat on your face" mistake you ever made on that topic and then work back to the "aha." Consider ways you can tap into funny stories about mistakes you made, false expectations you created, or other tough learning experiences you have had to educate the audience on why you are someone who can now teach them on that topic.

We know from experience that nothing is more interesting to your target audience than vulnerable, honest storytelling. If you can get past the misguided urge to present a perfect track record, you will grow your audience at a much quicker rate.

This kind of content also works tremendously well for email newsletters, since it's very difficult to get an audience to open them at a high rate. Best-selling author Jon Acuff writes one of our favorite email newsletters, and he does a great job with self-deprecation and vulnerability in his subject lines. A recent one arrived with this subject line: "The Personal Crisis That Changed My Life 12 Years Ago." That's going to be a pretty tough email not to open, isn't it?

When you open that email, you learn about how a business he started with a friend blew up in his face and taught him a lot about handling a crisis. He then turns the attention to how his audience can think about those lessons as they battle their own crises.

He could have just sent a newsletter with the headline "Five Ways to Navigate Crises," but because he got vulnerable with the headline, he ramped up both the number of opens and the impact.

Behind the Scenes/Personality-Driven Content

Few things build more trust and affinity with your audience than behind-the-scenes access to your life and/or personality.

This can include pictures from the road, humorous anecdotes, stories, and other personal content. Everyone has a different level of comfort sharing this kind of content, but one thing should be universally understood. The only reason for people to pay attention to your content instead of someone else's is that you bring something to the table that no one else can: *you.*

Both of us look for ways to weave in our own interests to the content we're creating, whether it is Clemson or Texas football, our pet peeves about air travel, funny family stories, or other behind-the-scenes content.

Don't overdo it, but this kind of content accomplishes two very important goals: 1) it keeps it fun for you, and 2) it allows your audience to get to know you as a person beyond "business"—and that, in turn, accelerates trust.

Earlier, we introduced you to Dr. Michelle Johnston, thought leader, executive coach, and business professor. She witnessed for herself how this kind of casual content can grab a huge audience—in this case, even more so than professionally designed content posts:

> I hired a social media company, and it was a great start because they taught me a lot. They said, "You know, the more you post, the better. You have to get over your discomfort, and you will." And so, I paid them to come up with a content media strategy for one post a week, and then once I kind of got used to it and realized my brand is all about connection, I figured I could do it myself.

> One of the things they liked doing, as any social media company does, is to package a post and make it really pretty so that my content looked good. But then I posted a candid picture of just me sending my daughter off to college, and I paralleled this to leadership. It now has 18,000 views. People can really relate when you show up as a human. That pretty, perfect little package of content doesn't get a whole lot of traction versus real personal connection with the users of LinkedIn.

Calls to Action

You-Driven content can also include calls to act upon things that benefit you, such as linking your audience to buy your book or to sign up for some event or activity. Part of being an authority is serving your audience with products and services that solve their problems.

However, you want to *not* overdo it in this category, or you'll fall victim to the ad-driven pitfall detailed earlier.

NEWS-DRIVEN CONTENT

Jacoby Jones had just scored to give the Ravens a 28–6 lead early in the second half of Super Bowl XLVII in 2013 in New Orleans.

Shortly after that touchdown, the lights went out in the Mercedes-Benz Superdome. It was pitch black in the stadium. The power outage interrupted television coverage of the game and stopped play for thirty-four minutes.

Tens of millions of people around the world were talking about this story, and in an instant, it provided brands with the first high-profile opportunity to take advantage of a tactic that has built significant momentum in content marketing: newsjacking.

Many brands tried their hands at it, but Oreo delivered the most talked-about tweet of the blackout, earning twelve thousand retweets in the first hour with a tweet that said "Power out? No problem," along with an image of a single Oreo on a dark, gradient background that read, "You can still dunk in the dark."

The tweet was noncontroversial, clearly brand connected, and very timely. In fact, it was so timely that agencies working for other brands were questioned in the year that followed about why they didn't have "Oreo hustle" in their work for them.

Oreo's tweet is a high-profile example of News-Driven content. The good news is that this category of content doesn't just work for big brands. It will work for you if it's a significant component of your personal content strategy.

You-Driven and Relationship-Driven content are primarily focused on serving those who already know you. To use another newspaper analogy, News-Driven content, by comparison, is your "front-page news" in terms of timeliness. It grabs attention from your audience more easily than other content because your target audience is already interested in this content (those who know you *and* those who don't). As such, News-Driven content gives you the best chance of all the categories to "go viral" in terms of the reach of that content.

News-Driven content is timely content that connects to a topic your target audience is paying attention to. There are two sub-categories of News-Driven content:

- **CALENDAR DRIVEN:** Although you can't predict what news will break in the future, you do have the ability to create an editorial calendar for the year based on the predictable calendar-driven news cycle. This is different in each niche, but global examples include holidays, tax season, a change of seasons, and so on. Think about the key dates/seasons for your target audience as it relates to your message, and ensure you're delivering super-timely content that lines up with those calendar-specific items. Although not as high profile as news-jacking, calendar-driven content is a great way to tie into your audience's attention. Think about what your target audience has front of mind throughout different times of the year, and use those predictable yearly areas of focus as a way to tailor your content.

- **NEWSJACKING:** As in the Oreo tweet, newsjacking connects your message to what's hot and happening in the news cycle, making your expertise extremely timely for your audience.

Because newsjacking is your best bet for going viral, we're going to go into more detail about what it is and how to use it effectively.

Our foreword writer, best-selling marketing author and speaker David Meerman Scott (there's that middle name again!) coined the term *newsjacking* all the way back in 2011, but it didn't get prime-time billing until the 2013 Super Bowl, and it didn't land on the *Oxford English Dictionary*'s (the OED's) short list for word of the year until 2017. The OED defined newsjacking as follows: "The practice of taking advantage of current events or news stories in such a way as to promote or advertise one's product or brand."

In their description for 2017 word-of-the year candidates, the OED provided more background on the term:

> In the space of a few short years, newsjacking has gone from an experimental technique to a staple in every social media–savvy marketing department's arsenal. Brands from across industry sectors fully embraced the strategy this year, increasingly taking advantage of current events to not only push their brand into the public consciousness but to align themselves with certain ethical or moral positions.
>
> Blending *news* and *hijacking*, the word itself dates back to the 1970s with reference to the theft of newspapers in order to sell them to scrap dealers. Its contemporary iteration, however, dates from the early twenty-first century, as first popularized by marketing and sales strategist David Meerman Scott's 2011 book, *Newsjacking: How to Inject Your Ideas into a Breaking News Story and Generate Tons of Media Coverage.*

It's interesting—David, by coining the word *newsjacking*, ended up newsjacking this story!

THE "WHY" OF NEWSJACKING

We often ask people to think about their digital platform as if it is their own media brand—or their newspaper, to continue that metaphor. Readers judge a media outlet by the value of its content and pay attention to those that entertain and inform them.

Although there is a place in your content strategy for You-Driven and Relationship-Driven content, the easiest way to grab an audience's attention is by connecting your content to what they are already paying attention to.

> **THE EASIEST WAY TO GRAB AN AUDIENCE'S ATTENTION IS BY CONNECTING YOUR CONTENT TO WHAT THEY ARE ALREADY PAYING ATTENTION TO.**

This doesn't mean the story you are "jacking" has to be national news like the Super Bowl blackout. It could be a niche story in your industry that your "who" is paying close attention to, such as a new research report, a regulatory shift, or other niche news. The important thing is to find a story that your target audience is gathered around and think of your newsjacking post as throwing up a flare to redirect their attention to your content.

When you "newsjack," we want you thinking like a *Wall Street Journal* op-ed columnist. You're not reporting the news—instead, we want you providing analysis, insight, or wit connected to the news your audience is already paying attention to.

When it comes to what to write about, think of the news your audience is worried about, anxious about, scared about, excited about, or otherwise monitoring. They are seeking analysis from experts on how they should react to that news and are more likely to give their attention to individual authorities they view as more trustworthy than institutions or larger media outlets. That's the opportunity here—to position yourself as someone your target audience can trust for insightful, timely analysis on the key issues affecting your industry.

Your target audience is much more likely to open an email newsletter, click on a link, or otherwise discover your content if it connects to something they are already actively seeking to learn more about. This is the reason that this category of content is the most likely to go viral—such articles are consumed and shared at a different level because of the timeliness and broadness of appeal—so, if you do it the right way, you put yourself in position to get monster results.

The other perk of this category? As you're about to discover, it frequently drives inbound PR and speaking opportunities.

WHEN SHOULD YOU NEWSJACK?

One of the most challenging components of newsjacking is getting the timing correct. A common mistake we see is people waiting a bit too long to connect their content to breaking news.

The ideal time to create content is within twenty-four to twenty-eight hours of a story breaking. This presents two challenges for leaders.

The first is the most obvious—as a busy leader, it's tough to find time to quickly create content in response to a breaking story (this is one reason a great ghostwriter is worth their weight in gold). The second is less obvious but more dangerous: newsjacking can be risky when done around controversial topics, and sometimes the urge to do something quickly can lead to a negative outcome if you're not careful.

In general, we want you to pay close attention to anything that gives you a "maybe this isn't the right move" feeling inside. When you get that emotional flare, listen to it.

At the same time, some of the best examples of high-profile news-jacking connect back to businesses doing very good things to help neighbors and clients surrounding very sensitive events.

One example is "Mattress Mack" in Houston, who opened up all his stores for displaced Houston residents to sleep in during Hurricane Harvey. He obviously didn't do this to create content or get clicks, but he generated the equivalent of millions in free PR and endeared himself to his city while helping hundreds in their time of need.

Another is Rocket Banners, a local sign company in Austin, which delivered "open for takeout" signs free of charge across the city as a way to help struggling restaurants during COVID-19. This cost Rocket Banners quite a bit of money at a time when business was almost certainly slow—but where do you think every single one of those restaurants is going to have signs printed in the future? The gesture also generated quite a bit of local media attention for the business, driving significant positive brand visibility.

We encourage you to think about newsjacking not just as a smart way to create content but also more broadly across your business as a way to overdeliver on value to your audience when they need it most.

DOES NEWSJACKING HAVE TO BE 100 PERCENT TAILORED TO THE NEWS?

This is one of the most common questions we get on newsjacking. The good news is that no, your newsjacking content doesn't have to be 100 percent focused on the news itself. Instead, we want you to focus on wrapping your content in the news story that your audience is already paying attention to.

If you look at many News-Driven posts, you'll see that the core content is really You-Driven. In other words, 80 percent of the article is focused on an evergreen perspective. You have a core belief system, framework, or perspective on your industry in place that you will be basing your authority on. One way to do that is to share that perspective generally.

That's not a bad thing to do, but it significantly limits the reach of that content. Instead, we want you to have your antennae up for news in your topic area that you can "wrap" around your content to ramp up the likelihood that

1. people read it,

2. people share it,

3. media discovers it, and

4. it gets significant viewership.

How can you give yourself the best chance to accomplish each of those outcomes? Borrow one of the primary mandates from the newspaper world: don't bury the lede!

Ensure the "title" for your content in an article, blog, video, or podcast includes a specific reference to the news story your audience is paying attention to. If possible, pair your post with a picture or graphic that is specifically connected to the news story as well. We're not sure if Oreo had a graphic designer on standby or if they just got lucky having that graphic already done, but their visual was spot on.

HOW CAN YOU USE NEWSJACKING TO DRIVE INBOUND PR?

The "traditional" media landscape has changed dramatically over the past decade, and layoffs have been the major theme.

As a result, there are fewer journalists covering more stories than ever before, and the last thing they have is time. They are so deluged with pitches and phone calls that often the best way to reach them is not by chasing them—it's by giving them a reason to chase you.

As counterintuitive as that sounds, consider this: except for dealing with publicists they know, media members are increasingly taking a "don't call us … we'll call you" approach to selecting the stories they will cover. This shift in the way media members operate has the potential to play right into the hands of leaders who understand it and widen their net to catch those queries.

When journalists search Google, Twitter, Forbes, or other content platforms looking for a subject matter expert on a certain topic, those published authors who have developed unique and interesting content rise to the top of the search results. This provides the expert with a great opportunity to not only provide their readers with great value but also position them to drive inbound PR opportunities.

Three things affect the likelihood that your timely post will attract valuable inbound media requests:

1. **TIMELINESS:** Again, you want to create your content as early in the life cycle of the story as possible and then share it widely.

2. **VISIBILITY:** If you post your News-Driven content on a large platform like *Forbes, Harvard Business Review,* or *HuffPost,* you have a higher likelihood of attracting top media to it based on the SEO those sites provide. Other things that affect visibility are keywords. Again, don't bury the timely connection in your blog post, as it will make it harder for search engines to pick up the connection. Instead, make sure you use the key terms in the blog title. Additionally, look for ways to raise the visibility of your content on LinkedIn and Twitter using targeted hashtags.

3. **PRESS ACCESSIBILITY:** If you do the first two things well, you may have a journalist trying to connect with you, but many people make it too hard for that to happen. It's not enough to have a contact form on your website—remember that most journalists are on deadline and need a source quickly, so they don't have much confidence that filling out your contact form is going to get them a timely answer. To counteract that, add a press tab on your website and include direct contact information for yourself or your publicity team. You can also include links to recent media hits and downloadable images related to you and your book. If you don't want to add a press tab, add a press contact on your contact page with your email and phone number to ensure a journalist can reach you easily if they want to. Have your publicity team directly pitch a journalist with your creative angle on a story related to a topic they cover or a story they are seeking resources for through one of the popular journalist databases.

The best way to generate PR in today's landscape is to have a two-pronged approach:

1. Work with a proven publicity firm that has existing media relationships that they can tap into to get above the noise and quickly deliver media opportunities for you.

2. Leverage News-Driven content to pull media inquiries your way as they look for subject matter experts online.

What we love about this approach is that it allows you to leverage the ongoing power of existing media outlets to grow your own audience moving forward.

WHY MUST YOUR CONTENT BE TIMELY?

We understand that this category of content is more high maintenance than the others based on the quick turn it requires you to make.

So ... why mess with it?

Beyond the many reasons we have already given in this book, maybe the most important is that thinking like the media requires you to compete with the media for your audience's attention.

Your audience increasingly puts every single content stream through the same filter they apply as consumers of media.

If consumers are not consistently getting value, they shift their attention somewhere else. They lose interest for an infinite number of reasons, but most often it is caused by an overreliance on You-Driven content. In other words, you're only serving up your own stuff. Yes, we want you serving up your own content, but we hope we've successfully made the case here for wrapping that content around a timely topic.

As consumers, we pay particular attention to certain individuals or brands because their content entertains and/or informs us. We get value from their content, and, in exchange, we give them something that truly matters in this information economy: our attention.

Just like it's easier to keep a client than acquire a new one, it's easier to keep the attention of an audience that is already tuned in to that topic than it is to redirect them to a topic they aren't yet paying attention to. In this world of micromedia, it doesn't take much for us to change the channel. Not only do we have more options—we also expect more than ever from those we pay attention to.

Again, think about what kind of newspaper you would value subscribing to. We certainly wouldn't subscribe to a newspaper filled with ads, selfies, or me-first content. We also wouldn't subscribe to a newspaper that is delivered without any consistency—once or twice a month just wouldn't cut it. We subscribe to newspapers that provide interesting and entertaining content on a consistent basis. They feature news we can use and put into practice that makes our lives better day to day.

News-Driven content will help you do just that, and we're excited to watch how it impacts the reach of your message—this year and beyond.

RELATIONSHIP-DRIVEN CONTENT

Now let's turn to our third category of content—Relationship-Driven.

The ability to build, sustain, and grow relationships is the basis of success and happiness in life.

We believe that this foundational truth also extends to success and happiness in business. In fact, most of us can trace the roots of our business success to a single relationship.

Adam cites the relationship with his mentor, Pat Williams, cofounder of the NBA's Orlando Magic, with providing the encouragement and vision that allowed him to start Advantage Media (which would later partner with Forbes to create Forbes Books) in 2005. In addition to being a sports executive, Pat is also a motivational speaker and a prolific author. Adam spent two summers working for a publishing house in high school, and he thought he would hate it. Turns out he actually liked it quite a bit. Right before he was to graduate from college, he was home in Orlando for a few days and had lunch with Pat. He convinced Adam that he should start a publishing company for professional speakers and business leaders. Pat believed there was a great need in the marketplace, and if not for his over-the-top encouragement, Adam's not sure that he would have taken the leap to start this business almost two decades ago.

That relationship was in small part luck (Adam growing up near Pat) and in large part intentionality (Adam nurturing the relationship through the years, including that fateful lunch that gave him the encouragement to get over the hump and buy that booth space at the National Speakers Association conference).

Can you trace your success in business back to a handful of relationships? Now think about how you built those relationships that provided that foundation. Were they built overnight? Were they transactional in nature? Of course not—relationships like that are built over time and grow based on a foundation of mutual trust built between parties.

But what's fascinating when you look back at your most seminal business relationships are the simple ways in which they started, such as the following:

- Sitting next to a future strategic partner at a conference or on a plane

- Growing up next door to a successful businessperson

- Getting introduced to a future monster client at a cocktail party

These relationship-building starting points used to happen only in person, and for many business leaders, they still do. They also used to be mostly left up to happenstance or luck. But relationship building doesn't have to be confined to nonscalable in-person efforts and certainly not fate.

Approach building an Authority Advantage not only as an opportunity to build your brand but also as a bridge to build and strengthen relationships with others. By doing so, you give yourself a clear road map to creating and growing relationships at a scale and speed you may not realize is possible.

Let's start with scale.

In today's digital environment, relationships that used to start in person can now begin online by, for example, the following:

- Trading tweets with a journalist who will go on to interview you dozens of times at top media outlets

- Interviewing a prospect on your podcast who will go on to buy six figures' worth of services over the next two years

- Quoting a client in your *Forbes* column who will use it as a reason to refer you to others

The other multiplier on relationship building is the speed with which you can establish trust when you build your authority. As noted earlier, trust used to take years and years to build in an offline environment but now is accelerated significantly when you lead with authority for your brand online.

It starts with understanding the big picture of Relationship-Driven content.

THE MAGIC OF RELATIONSHIP-DRIVEN CONTENT

We talk often about the importance of thinking of yourself as a media outlet as you begin creating content. One of the foundations of good media is that they don't typically limit their content to their own perspective. They rely on the expertise of others to curate the best possible content for their audience.

When you involve other people in your content, you not only build a relationship with them, but you also give them a reason to direct their audience into your stadium. Content marketing at its best is a relationship-building tool. As discussed earlier, it empowers you to create and strengthen relationships at a scale and speed not previously possible.

Mike Maddock, a thought leader you may remember from chapter 4 (he's the guy in the jeans!), puts it like this:

> The best authority folks spend more time posting about other people than themselves. In other words, they go looking for someone in their network that they're really impressed with. Something they did, something they say, and they repost that. That's a discipline that I think gets lost on people that are trying to promote a book or their own authority. It's like, "Look at me, look at me, look at me—see, I'm smart."
>
> There's a John Wooden quote, the legendary UCLA coach: "Show me your friends and I'll show you your future." You can telegraph who you are by who you're hanging with and who you're posting about. And social media allows you to do that. And I think that's a better strategy than just posting about yourself all the time or your new book or whatever.

Let's say we were all sitting in our conference room in Charleston, South Carolina, working together to build a personalized MAP for you, and we asked you to write the names of the fifty people who will make the biggest difference in the growth of your business over the next three to five years on our whiteboard. Our guess is, we could complete that list. The names on the whiteboard are likely to be split between people you know (existing clients, strategic partners, and other important connections) and people you want to know but don't currently (potential clients, potential strategic partners, influencers, and others). Imagine that we drew a line down the middle of the whiteboard and separated the two groups with roughly twenty-five people in each.

Once we have those names on the whiteboard, the next question from you is likely to be "Okay, great. Now what? How do I build and strengthen relationships with this group beyond the obvious tactics?"

The obvious tactics are ones you're familiar with. For existing relationships, the typical approach to strengthening them and generating new leads (beyond doing a great job for them) involves thank-you gifts, wine tastings, and other events. Or, worst of all, simply asking for referrals. There's nothing wrong with these tactics (other than asking for referrals), but they typically limit the impact to nonscalable outcomes.

In pursuit of new relationships, it's typically targeted outbound emails or calls seeking a Zoom session or meeting to discuss potential areas of opportunity. As business leaders, we're all familiar with these requests because we get hundreds of them a week and can't delete them quickly enough.

But when you approach such relationships with a slight shift, everything changes about both the response and the goodwill built as a result.

What is the shift?

We want you to be seen not as someone with something to sell but as someone with something to teach. Curious how to make this happen? Let's unpack it.

> **BE SEEN NOT AS SOMEONE WITH SOMETHING TO SELL BUT AS SOMEONE WITH SOMETHING TO TEACH.**

WHEN DONE RIGHT, CONTENT MARKETING = BUSINESS DEVELOPMENT

Let's go back to our list of fifty growth-focused relationships. What if, instead of pushing your requests at them, you instead led with *value* for them? When you do that, you're not asking for something (delete!)—you're leading with a win for them.

How do you offer them a win?

Few things mean more to business leaders than getting featured in the media or a book. This could be a mention in *Forbes*, an interview on your podcast, or a spotlight in your book. When you publish a book, start a podcast, or begin writing a column or blog, you position yourself as a member of the media with something to teach—not as an operator with something to sell.

The magic in this approach is not just in catching the relationship target's attention; it's also in the following three areas:

1. Assuming you are only interviewing smart people with good ideas, your audience is going to benefit from the content.

2. You're changing the nature of your interaction with that prospect or potential strategic partner. In a normal sales meeting or sales call where you're in a salesperson versus prospect dynamic, you have a huge hill to climb. By comparison, when you interview someone, it becomes a peer-to-peer interaction, which gives you a much more authoritative position.

3. You're giving your interviewee a reason to share the link to your website, article, or interview once it runs. To go back to the stadium analogy, you're inviting that person onto your stage, and they're bringing their audience into your stadium with them when they share it.

WHAT SUCCESS WITH RELATIONSHIP-DRIVEN CONTENT LOOKS LIKE

We worked with a marketing agency based in Atlanta that was trying to generate attention from CMOs of Fortune 1000 companies in the area. Not an easy task, to say the least, and they had not been very successful with traditional outbound sales tactics.

They embraced this mindset of thinking more like the media than a marketer and went a step further than most do—they built a podcast studio in their office. Their goal was not just to get their target customer to come on the podcast—their goal was to have a reason to get the target CMO into their office to do the podcast interview so they could witness their culture firsthand and get a feel for the agency.

They began reaching out to target CMOs and inviting them on the podcast—and the response rate was remarkable. Previously, they couldn't get calls returned, and now they were having peer-to-peer conversations with these CMOs on their terms and in their office, all the while building goodwill with them. They went on to close significant business with two of the companies they engaged and built goodwill across the board.

But Relationship-Driven content isn't limited to a formal interview series. In fact, it can be woven into every piece of content you create.

Let's look at the various forms of Relationship-Driven content and how you can implement them moving forward.

HOW TO USE RELATIONSHIP-DRIVEN CONTENT

There are numerous ways to use Relationship-Driven content. Here are the tactics we encourage you to use:

1.) *Start an Interview Series*

Have you ever thought about using an interview series as a door-opening tool?

One of the fastest-growing regional banks in Texas did, and it changed everything about the way they approach business development and referral marketing.

When you walk into their new branch in downtown Austin, you see a lot of the same things you would see at most bank branches—teller spots, offices, and yes, free coffee. But one thing is going to stand out to you when you look to the left—a podcast studio.

Have you ever been to a bank with a podcast studio in the lobby? What's it doing there?

The bank realized that every other bank in Austin was doing exactly the same thing to open doors: "Let's go play golf or grab drinks or hit up a networking lunch." These are tough ways to grind out new relationships.

This bank decided they could give themselves the Authority Advantage by doing something completely different. Instead of reaching out and asking for something (maybe their most valuable item—time!), they reached out with a win for the leader they were targeting: "Hey, we're fans of what you and your company are doing. We would love to have you as a guest on an upcoming episode of our podcast."

They found that several things happened as a result. That leader was highly likely to respond to that email in a positive manner and excitedly come into that new bank branch for their podcast interview. And, at worst, a new relationship is built. What we've seen happen time and time again is that this interview becomes the starting point for the opportunity to quote future business, generate referrals, and other results of the goodwill built.

Back to your whiteboard of the fifty connections you expect to be most helpful to your business—we want your interview series to build and strengthen those connections. Use your podcast as both a way to empower those who already know and love you to share your content as well as a method to open doors with people you are seeking to build a relationship with á la the bank and marketing agency we just discussed.

So, rather than sending the typical outbound email to prospects, you instead send an email to them letting them know you're a fan of their work (assuming you are—more on this below) and you'd like to invite them to be a guest on your podcast.

The invitation should look something like this:

Subject: Interview request ~ Forbes Books Audio "Culture Matters" Podcast

Dear Sharon,

I hope you're having a great week.

I have been a longtime fan of the work you and your team do at Acme Brick Company. I host a podcast on the Forbes Books Audio Podcast Network titled "Culture Matters," and I would love to have you as a guest on an upcoming episode to discuss your approach to culture at Acme and lessons learned along the way.

Recent guests on my podcast have been executives from IBM, Deloitte, and Amazon, so you'd be in good company. Here's a link to find those and other past episodes, in case you're curious.

If you're game for an interview, please let me know, and I'll send more details over.

Thanks,

Kathy

Think about the power of this email as a door opener for your business.

Your sales team has been trying to get their foot in the door with Acme for the past several years but can't seem to crack the code. You have just bypassed the gatekeepers and gone directly to the CEO with an email she can't open quickly enough based on the subject line. She may not have heard of you, but the association with Forbes and those you have recently interviewed elevate this request to something she's eagerly ready to accept.

This focuses your time on best and highest use (building and strengthening strategic relationships) while also creating content your audience will find valuable.

Here are a couple of useful things to think about as it relates to your interview series:

- **FOCUS:** The magic in a good interview series is that it allows you to focus only on relationship targets. The time spent has value whether or not a huge audience is built based on the crossover with business development. Again—worry less about the size of the listening audience and more about the fifty relationships you're nurturing with the podcast.

- **RESIST THE URGE TO BAIT AND SWITCH:** The interview series loses all its impact if it is perceived as a sales tactic. Again, you need to be viewed as a member of the media (which you are when you have a podcast), so don't angle in with any kind of pitch as part of the interaction. Instead, leverage the peer-to-peer environment that an interview facilitates to further cement your authority. Following the interview, you can send a follow-up note and perhaps even a signed copy of your book as a thank-you, but you want to let them take the first step in terms of requesting more information, which they often will.

- **FORMAT:** Although some leaders choose to do their interview series via text content in the form of a blog post, we recommend either a podcast or a video interview series as the target format because both facilitate a more intimate connection with the relationship target.

- **CREATE COLLATERAL TO EMPOWER SHARING:** Once the interview is done, the next step is to make it as easy as possible for your guest to share the link and promote it to their list.

Once you design your initial interview graphics, they are very easy to edit and update with each new guest you have on.

If you do nothing else with your content strategy in the future than start and consistently execute an interview series with high-value relationships and high-value targets, you'll move meaningfully in the direction of your business growth goals.

2.) *Involve Others in News-Driven and You-Driven Content*

As a general rule, the more other people you can involve in your content strategy, the quicker your audience and impact will grow.

Let's say your PR team comes to you with a request to write a guest blog for *Forbes*. First of all, congrats! But once the excitement wears off, the next question is this: How can you get the most value from this opportunity?

One way to get value from this opportunity is to share eight hundred to one thousand words of your own perspective. Another way to use this opportunity that will provide many multiples of value over that first option is to think about who else you can quote, feature, or mention in your article as a way to build goodwill with them and provide a more interesting article for *Forbes*.

Think about sending this kind of email to your biggest referral partner:

> **Subject: Interview for a Forbes piece?**
>
> Hi Jim,
>
> Hope all is well in Dallas!
>
> I am working on a blog for Forbes on leading through crisis, and I thought of your journey this year and would love to get a quote or two about how you navigated the pandemic with your consulting business. Do you have time Thursday for a chat?
>
> Thanks,
>
> Mark

We want Jim thinking two things after reading this email:

1. "Wow—I had no idea Mark writes for Forbes!"

2. "I'm incredibly grateful he thought of me for an interview."

Once the article runs, Jim is going to promote the hell out of it because it makes him look good for being quoted in *Forbes*, and as he promotes it, he's going to talk to his audience about how awesome Mark is.

Ideally, you could quote three to five different people per article or blog and use it to both nurture existing relationships (à la Jim and Mark) and to build new relationships.

Perhaps the most important multiplier here for relationships is the other party viewing you not as someone with something to sell but as a member of the media/authority. When you start with that kind of peer-to-peer interaction, you put yourself in a position to sell much more than you would otherwise.

3.) *Leverage Social Media to Build and Strengthen Relationships*

One of the most effective and efficient ways to give your audience valuable content and build relationships with journalists, key influencers, and current/potential relationships in your space is to share their content and tag them along the way. We do not want you to situate yourself as a "fan" when you do this. Go above and beyond simply commenting, "Great post!" Instead, do this in a peer-to-peer way, adding commentary that only an authority in the shared space could add.

For example—let's say you're up early on a Sunday morning reading the paper and you see a client featured in the paper. Consider taking five or ten extra minutes to tag them on Twitter and LinkedIn with a link to the article or piece of coverage. This sounds small, but it has a big impact on those you're putting in the spotlight.

Another way to think about this is to start a series on Facebook, LinkedIn, or Twitter where every week you put a spotlight on a local business, nonprofit, or organization that you think your audience should be paying attention to. Whether that audience pays attention or not, those organizations you feature will view it as a significant act of goodwill, and it will pull them closer to you.

4.) *Involve Others in Your Book*

We're going to explore the many doors publishing your own book will open for you in the earned media section of this book, but many authors make the mistake of filling their book with only You-Driven content—their story, their perspective, their ideas, or their intellectual property. Those are all things we want in your book, but we also want to include those same things from as many other people from your whiteboard list of fifty as possible.

Dr. Michelle Johnston did just that with her Forbes Book best-seller, *The Seismic Shift of Leadership,* and it helped her expand her network to a tremendous level:

> I'm an executive coach in addition to being a management professor, and I was coaching leaders who I could see were actively getting pushed out of their organization ... because they would not let go of the command-and-control style.[4] And it was creating cultures of fear. It was just not working. I really wanted to help, but I was trying to figure out, *Okay, what's going on?* I thought, *Well, let me interview global leaders, successful leaders who have figured it out.* That in turn led me to see this process was all about connection. My sphere of influence as an academic and a coach was pretty small at the time. It was definitely like a lightning bolt.

The most successful books we publish are the ones that generate the most business, independence, and impact for our authors. The best way to generate those results as an author is to use your book to both open doors with target relationships and empower those you already know to want to talk about the book. You do both of those things when you include others in your book.

It's a big deal to write a book. It's also a big deal to be featured in a book, and we encourage you not to discount the impact it can have on others. In fact, we have numerous clients who generate an ROI before their book is ever published based on using this principle.

---

4   Authors' note: This is the same type of leader that we termed "The Top-Down Leader" in chapter 3.

BE SMART ABOUT RELATIONSHIP-DRIVEN CONTENT

While the first two categories of content (You-Driven and News-Driven) are important, the biggest game changer in terms of traction, impact, and—to be frank—fun is the third category: Relationship-Driven content.

When you have a media mindset, you are comfortable enough in your own authority to curate content from others as a way to build relationships and give value to your audience. While You-Driven content and News-Driven content will both make an impact over time, Relationship-Driven content can make an impact immediately based on the scale and trust multipliers it provides.

> CONTENT MARKETING … IF YOU CAN EMBRACE IT, YOU WILL BE PLAYING A GAME NO ONE ELSE KNOWS IS BEING PLAYED.

Content marketing, when used the right way, is a great bridge to new relationships. But it's a rare mindset that sees that and utilizes it. If you can embrace it, you will be playing a game no one else knows is being played.

CONDUCT A CONTENT AUDIT

Now that you understand that your content should be evenly split across the three categories we mentioned in this section (You-Driven, News-Driven, and Relationship-Driven), we encourage you to go back and do an audit of your current content streams across each of your channels (from video to text to audio to pictures).

Our expectation is that your content probably leans most heavily into the You-Driven category. However, as Mike says, and as we have seen with many other leaders, the fun of creating content is involving others in it. By doing this, you put a spotlight on other leaders, curate insights for your audience, and open doors that lead to new opportunities. As you move forward, diversify your content equally across the three categories discussed in this chapter to create the biggest upside.

PART THREE

THE NEW MEDIA LANDSCAPE

UNDERSTANDING TODAY'S MEDIA CATEGORIES AND HOW TO LEVERAGE THEM TO BUILD AUTHORITY

CHAPTER NINE:

THE KEY TO UNDERSTANDING MEDIA TODAY

WE WERE CRUSHING IT.

It was 2013, and the golden era of organic reach for brands and marketers was in full force on Facebook.

Just a few years before, we had launched a Facebook company page for a globally recognized brand and built the audience into the millions. The size of the audience, coupled with the huge organic reach Facebook provided to brands at the time, resulted in massive traffic (and sales) for our client and the biggest retainer our agency had at the time. We continued to grow that audience and enjoy that reach for several years—until a very dark day changed everything for marketers in the fall of 2013.

Facebook initiated their first major algorithm shift.

Prior to that shift, Facebook intentionally worked to get brands fat and happy by reaching a huge audience on real estate they owned. They did this by giving free and open access, *at first,* to brands that launched their new business pages on the site.

In doing so, they conditioned those brands to the results that came from accessing such a large audience—until they flipped a switch with that algorithm change, essentially telling brands, "Congrats—you have built a big audience on your page, but guess what? That audience is standing on dirt that we own, and if you want to continue reaching them, you're going to start paying to sponsor posts."

Facebook was the first to pull this bait and switch on brands, but it set the course for future social media platforms, including LinkedIn, Instagram, Twitter, and others, to do exactly the same thing. In fact, they were writing a playbook that social media platforms continue to follow to this day:

- **STEP 1**: Attract a large audience to the social media platform by providing a great user experience.

- **STEP 2**: Give companies and advertisers a taste of the impact they can have by getting active on the platform by providing large organic (free) reach.

- **STEP 3**: Once brands have gathered a large audience of real estate the social media platform owns, and once those brands are accustomed to a certain amount of reach, shift the algorithm to limit that reach *unless they pay for it.* That payment can be a direct one to the platform or an indirect cost to your organization, because even organic search results require you to invest in the things that the platform decides are important—and those things change, requiring you to revamp your assets to comply. Some of this cannot be avoided if we want the discoverability that almost all brands need to grow and reinforce trust/credibility.

The algorithms that drive attention on the world's most visited social media channels have come under attack recently from just about everyone—from the EU to Elon Musk. To be clear, these algorithms are often not your friend, particularly when it comes to leveraging the audiences you've built on these platforms.

Without question the most common mistake we see in what we call "rented media" (more on that later) is people and brands amassing a huge audience on real estate they don't own (like the social media sites) and being content to leave that audience there. This creates a barrier between you and your audience that gives a platform leverage over you.

Don't fall into this trap.

Instead, in this section of the book we're going to show you what the current lay of the land is in terms of media. Then we will show you how to strategically leverage visibility on rented and earned media to drive your audience back to real estate you own so that you control the connection.

THE NEW MEDIA LANDSCAPE AND VIRTUAL REAL ESTATE

Seismic shifts in the media landscape are old news at this point, but one thing is clear—they set up a great environment for those who understand and leverage them and a frustrating (not to mention expensive) environment for those who don't.

The key to understanding the new media landscape is to develop a keen understanding of virtual real estate and, more specifically, a clear grasp of who "owns" the connection to the audience you're communicating with. In years past, the biggest landowner in terms of audience size was traditional media. If you wanted to reach their large audience, you had to either rent their platform by buying an ad or be fortunate enough to earn your way via an interview or feature.

In recent years, power has shifted toward the largest rented media brands in the world: Google, as well as Facebook, TikTok, LinkedIn, Twitter, Instagram, and other large social media platforms, who, as we just discussed, are following a proven playbook that firmly plants them between you and your customer base. Their ultimate goal is to make you pay them for that access.

As you might imagine, the recipe for success is not ignoring rented or earned media. After all, they currently give you access to huge audiences. Instead, we believe you should consider the smartest strategies for these platforms and then drive people back to real estate that's yours—so *you* own the connection with them.

The ability to do this efficiently and effectively is relatively new. In the previous media era, not only did traditional media "own" the largest swaths of audience, but it was also more difficult to siphon off that audience and drive them back to land that you, the authority, owned. Generally, that effort was aimed at getting them to join a physical mailing list, which caused considerable friction for your audience.

As a result, large companies with big budgets had a significant advantage—because smaller companies or individuals couldn't afford to build authority or give themselves enough leverage in their market by owning the connection to their audience. In other words, outside of amassing a physical mailing list, which was difficult to build and expensive to reach consistently, you couldn't be "the media." You had to go through them.

Fast-forward to today. We still have rented and earned media, but the biggest shift in terms of lead generation (and leverage) is the growth of *owned media* beyond the physical mailing list. When you own the connection to your audience, you remove barriers between you and your audience, and that gives you vital leverage ahead of continued shifts in the landscape.

> WHEN YOU OWN THE CONNECTION TO YOUR AUDIENCE, YOU REMOVE BARRIERS BETWEEN YOU AND YOUR AUDIENCE.

Here's what the new media landscape looks like:

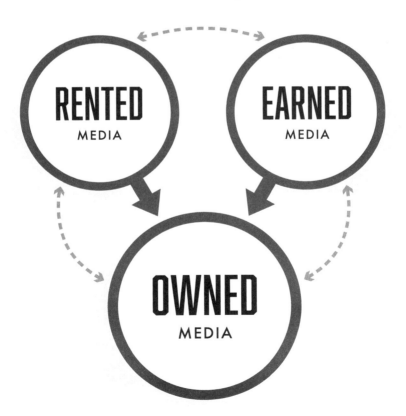

This *Rented, Earned, and Owned Media* framework was initially put forth in *Mastering the New Media Landscape: Embrace the Micromedia Mindset* (Berrett-Koehler, 2016), which Rusty coauthored with Barbara Cave Henricks, and these may be terms you have heard before. However, in our experience, these categories are likely terms you have heard before, but most leaders don't have a clear understanding of how they relate to each other and, more importantly, how to best leverage each for maximum impact. In the next few chapters, we're going to take a deep dive on each kind of media and show you how to integrate them to create your Authority Advantage.

10

RENTED MEDIA

WE STARTED OFF this section of the book by ragging on Facebook and other social media platforms, but the reality is that rented media is a great tool to leverage in the post media landscape to expand your reach and make a bigger impact.

But it's a double-edged sword.

As noted, although it's great to build an audience via social media, the longer you leave your audience there, the more beholden you are to that particular social media channel's willingness to let you access that audience. In short, you are essentially building a crowd on land someone else owns, and who knows how much they will want to charge you to access that crowd in the future?

THE FOCUS FOR YOUR RENTED MEDIA STRATEGY NEEDS TO BE ON PROVIDING VALUE TO YOUR AUDIENCE AND THEN DRIVING THEM BACK TO REAL ESTATE YOU OWN.

To be clear, we're not suggesting that you steer clear of rented media as you build authority. In fact, it's quite the opposite. But you need to have your eyes wide open that any audience you build on real estate someone else owns is as much yours as a house you rent. As we discussed earlier, the focus for your rented media strategy needs to be on providing value to your audience and then driving them back to real estate you own.

WHAT IS RENTED MEDIA?

When most leaders hear us advocate for building a more visible and authentic personal brand and creating an Authority Advantage, they immediately think of the rented media content category. Rented media includes all media where you fully control the content, but you don't own the real estate, including the following:

- Advertising
- Social media channels (your LinkedIn account, Facebook page, etc.)
- Bio pages on corporate sites
- Third-party listings at sites like Crunchbase, Doximity, or Healthgrades

One reality of rented media is that it doesn't provide you with much authority, because the audience knows the barrier to entry is incredibly low. After all, anyone with a budget and an internet connection can buy an ad or start a Twitter account.

But what it lacks in credibility and leverage, it makes up in scale and the ability to hypertarget your audience if managed correctly.

BUILDING YOUR RENTED MEDIA STRATEGY

Even though most people lump social media channels together into one category, it's crucial to understand that each social media channel has its own nuances and etiquette. We believe it's helpful to look at social media channels as if they sit on a spectrum. On one end of the spectrum are relationship-sustaining channels. These are channels where the etiquette is such that users are there to stay in touch with people and brands they already know.

Facebook lives firmly at this end of the spectrum, as most people are not there to take chances on new companies and potential friends. It's just not the culture of that platform. That doesn't mean that well-targeted advertising campaigns to "future fans" won't work. They can. It just means that it is extremely hard to build an organic audience to a "fan" page until people know to look for you.

On the other end of the spectrum, you'll find "relationship-building" channels where the etiquette is such that we're there to have conversations with people we may or may not know about topics that we have a shared interest in. Twitter sits firmly at that end of the spectrum. Instagram sits near Twitter, as its platform is also wide open for conversations and connections surrounding hashtags that connect people with like-minded interests who may not have previously known each other.

LinkedIn used to live on the far-right side of the spectrum with Facebook. It was a platform we spent time on for one of two sporadic reasons—because we were either looking for a job or looking to hire someone for an open position. LinkedIn recognized that the main utility of their platform was built around a "transactional" utility that kept our attention away from its real estate for long periods of time, and they have done a tremendous job (especially postacquisition from Microsoft) of reinventing the experience for its users.

Years ago, LinkedIn made one of the most impressive shifts any large social media platform has made when it decided to pivot from a job-hunting platform to a content-marketing platform. It then began implementing a strategy focused on helping you envision your LinkedIn profile as your professional home base, which is in many ways what it is today.

We don't have room in this book to provide a specific game plan for each and every social media platform. However, because LinkedIn is the most common search result when you Google a leader's name, and because most readers of this book will get the biggest benefit from LinkedIn, we want to look at what you can do to make sure your LinkedIn presence is working for you.

DEEP DIVE ON LINKEDIN: WHAT'S CHANGED, AND HOW YOU CAN WIN

The first and most important shift that LinkedIn made was a move from the old résumé/CV-style profile to the current version (as we're writing this book), which looks more like the homepage of a website than anything else. LinkedIn recognized that it could earn more of our attention by empowering users to create a home base as a professional that looked more dynamic than its old-style pseudorésumé format.

The first level in success on LinkedIn is fully building out your static profile. The current LinkedIn profile design at the time of this writing is a dynamic interface that you can do a lot with. For many leaders who don't yet have a home base personal-brand website in place, your LinkedIn profile may be the very first image that is created in the minds of your audience. As a result, you want to make sure you create a very intentional impression.

Here are a few key components to a successful static profile:

- **VISUALS:** You have the ability to get very visual with your profile, specifically with the following images:

  - ❑ **HEADER IMAGE:** The header image is the horizontal image at the top of the profile. It's amazing how many profiles we view that either don't have any header image in place or have some generic beach picture that does nothing for the image in the mind of the person visiting your profile. Similar to the header image we push you toward on your website, think about authority by association and how you can use the most impressive authority-building visual you have in place. This might be a picture of you speaking publicly, being interviewed in the media, or perhaps accepting an award. You want something that positions you as someone with something to teach.

  - ❑ **AVATAR PROFILE IMAGE:** You don't need to do anything too dynamic here other than featuring a current quality image of yourself that is consistent with the image you want to project.

  - ❑ **BIO IMAGES/VIDEOS:** As you'll read about below, LinkedIn now gives you the ability to showcase a full narrative bio in addition to the old-style résumé view that is still somewhat intact at the bottom of your profile. As part of your bio, you can now upload pictures and videos and also link out to high-value articles or other media coverage. We encourage you to upload speaking videos, showcase high-quality still images, and link viewers to the three to five most impressive media hits you have in place. If you have written a book, make sure to link to it on Amazon as well. We'll talk about real-time videos and images a bit later in this chapter, but make sure your static images are working for you.

❑ **LOGOS:** One commonly ignored visual component of your LinkedIn profile are the logos that correspond to your work experience. Many entrepreneurs make the mistake of featuring their company as part of their experience but don't have a formal company page, which means that no logo shows up as part of the feature. This can give the wrong impression to your target audience—that you may not have a real business or that it's too small to have a company page. Go the extra step of setting up a company page complete with a logo to ensure you make the right impression on your audience.

• **TEXT:** As with anything else online, the visuals make the first impression for you. We want to make sure that once your audience is "hooked" with the right images, the text found on your profile reinforces your authority. But the right words are also important. Here are the key text components to your static profile:

❑ **YOUR NAME:** Sounds pretty basic, right? And it is, as long as the name listed is consistent with your "brand name." We have talked at length in this book about the importance of "owning" your brand name. Ensure that the name listed on your LinkedIn profile includes your middle initial, middle name, and/or full version of your first name. It's very tactical but also an unforced error in terms of search engine optimization if the name you have listed isn't consistent. We see it far too often.

❑ **YOUR HEADLINE:** You may have heard this called a "one-liner," but it is the one-line description featured right next to your name. It's incredibly important not only because it gives the viewer a quick glance of who you are and what you do but also because it travels with your picture and name anywhere you appear on LinkedIn (in search results, next to an article you write, etc.). Instead of using it purely for a factual title (financial advisor or entrepreneur or dentist), make it work for you by packing in a more descriptive headline. Here is an example:

Best-Selling Author and Keynote Speaker | CEO at Smith Media | Passionate about ROI-Driven Marketing | Entrepreneur #EO

❑ **YOUR BIO:** As mentioned above, one of the biggest changes LinkedIn made to static profiles is shifting from a pure résumé style to one that now combines both narrative bio and your résumé. Remember that the first image you create with your audience may very well be on LinkedIn, so we want the same high-quality bio that is developed for your website featured on LinkedIn. Take time to combine trust-building authority by association with mission-driven thought leadership for maximum impact.

❑ **YOUR WORK EXPERIENCE AND EDUCATION:** The résumé-style component of your static profile allows you to list all your work and education experience. In most cases, the description for well-known universities and businesses with a presence on LinkedIn will autopopulate a description, which is great. For any businesses you own, take the time to provide some sizzle.

Once you update the visuals and text within your profile, the good news is that you can leave it alone for a while. We recommend auditing your static profile once every quarter to add in new images, update your bio, and make any other changes that are needed.

By the way, much of the advice we're giving for LinkedIn applies across your social media channels, such as your header image on Twitter or your name on Instagram. Make sure you are consistent, and lead with visuals that establish credibility with those who don't yet know you.

CONNECTIONS AND THE RISE OF THE BUSINESS INFLUENCER

Although LinkedIn wants you to think of your profile as your home base as a professional, make sure you keep crystal clear that your home base is your "owned media" (to be discussed in chapter 12). This begins with your website and continues with your email and/or mailing list. Although to you, LinkedIn is rented media, it's a different story for LinkedIn itself, to whom your profile and its platform are its owned media. As such, LinkedIn's goal is to keep your attention, your content, and your audience on its real estate so it can monetize each. To do so much more effectively than it used to, several years ago

LinkedIn made the same decision we're pushing you to make with your own mindset. It decided it would become a media outlet.

Put simply, LinkedIn grew tired of us clicking on links and leaving its real estate to head to *Forbes, Fast Company, Harvard Business Review*, YouTube, and other platforms to read, watch, and consume business-related content. It recognized that it was a very good point of discovery for such content, but to generate more revenue, it also needed to become a point of consumption for such content. In other words, LinkedIn wanted to facilitate the creation of the exact same type of business content we can read on top business media websites, except they didn't want to pay a bunch of journalists to create it. Instead, they built out a very savvy editorial team and decided to leave the responsibility of creating the content to the cheapest, most eager workforce they had access to: *you.*

To be a bit more specific, the LinkedIn "Influencer" program actually started with a hundred influencers hand selected by the editorial board (yes, a real human editorial board!). That curated list included President Obama, Richard Branson, and numerous other global authorities. After limiting "long-form" content creation to this group for the first phase of the program, LinkedIn eventually opened its publishing platform to every single user on the site. In doing so, LinkedIn not only dramatically ramped up the volume of native content on its real estate but also for the first time opened up the opportunity for you to build an audience beyond connections.

Keep in mind that LinkedIn continues to have a human editorial team, which, as of 2023, numbers around two hundred people around the globe. Their curation of key stories and hashtags gives LinkedIn not only a key differentiator among social media platforms but also dramatically enhances opportunities for leaders to create content on LinkedIn that catches their eye.

TO CONNECT OR NOT TO CONNECT?

As you may know, for many years the only way to build an audience on LinkedIn was to formally connect with other LinkedIn users. However, now LinkedIn users have the ability to "follow" you on the site, which means they receive alerts when you have published something even though they aren't a formal connection.

We don't recommend accepting connection requests from people on LinkedIn unless you truly know them, because when you do that, your new connection now has the ability to reach your connections through you, and you'll be seen as the point of reference. In other words, if I'm looking to sell life insurance and I see that you have a bunch of high-quality connections, I might send you a connection request to see if you'll accept. If you do, I can now start sending messages to your LinkedIn connections pitching my products, and they will see that you are the only shared connection in place. In other words, you'll be seen as the reason they're getting the note from this sales rep.

We do want you to accept any and all connection requests from people you truly do know. Such connections provide one of the most significant blends of earned and rented media that exists in today's media landscape. When we view your profile on LinkedIn, we can see whether or not we have any shared connections. Then, when we see you are connected with people we know and respect, it provides you with a sort of indirect endorsement from those people. The shared relationship accelerates the speed of trust in a similar way that an in-person introduction from a mutual friend at a networking event does.

But as valuable as that indirect endorsement is, it works in the opposite direction when we see you're connected with someone we don't respect. Therefore, watch your connections closely, and limit them to people you know and respect. For everyone else, we want you to be creating the kind of content on LinkedIn that is worth following, and we want your "follower" count to be as large as possible.

LEVERAGING GREAT CONTENT TO BUILD YOUR PRESENCE ON LINKEDIN

This book has explored what a great content strategy looks like at length, but we do want to highlight a few items to think about as you grow your presence on the platform.

LinkedIn has recently created a strategic distinction between thought leaders (content contributors) and workforce learners (content consumers), and the key public acknowledgement of this is their option to turn your profile to "Creator Mode" (as of the writing of this book, this is available for profiles of more than two thousand connections). This allows the platform to position profile content more effectively to the user base and puts you in position to grow your audience more rapidly. Additionally, many expect that we will see paid subscription content in all forms (written, podcast, video, etc.) coming around the corner as well.

We like to sort content on LinkedIn into two big picture categories outside of your static bio and one-to-one messaging: Short-form content and long-form content. While both content categories filter into your main LinkedIn newsfeed, there are large differences between the two.

Short-Form Content

When you log on to LinkedIn, you see a general news feed that has many similarities to other social media news feeds (particularly Facebook and Twitter). At the top, you'll have a prompt to "start a post," which then offers you the chance to share a picture, video, or text update (including linking to external content). Right under that prompt is another prompt to "write an article on LinkedIn," which we'll discuss more in the section below on long-form content.

When you share something in the short-form category on LinkedIn, the same content strategy we talked about earlier applies. First of all, you want to involve as many others as possible for maximum reach and relationship building. Secondly, the more topical the content, the better. Thirdly, the more visual the content, the better.

Here are a few things to remember when it comes to short-form content on LinkedIn:

- **VISUALS ALWAYS WIN.** Whether it's a fantastic picture or—even better—a quick video, your content is going to be seen by many more people on LinkedIn when you pair it with a good image.

- **WHEN POSTING VIDEO, ALWAYS DO IT NATIVELY.** Remember that LinkedIn's algorithm is built to reinforce behaviors that keep attention on its own real estate. As such, if you shoot a great video and upload it to YouTube before sharing the link on LinkedIn, you can expect to receive very little reach from that video (because your post is taking LinkedIn users off LinkedIn to watch it). Instead, upload the video directly to LinkedIn for far more reach from LinkedIn's algorithm.

- **INVOLVE OTHERS IN YOUR CONTENT.** Content marketing at its best is a relationship-building vehicle, and short-form content on LinkedIn is a tremendous way to do that. Don't underestimate the power of a "like" or a comment on a work anniversary, career announcement, or other short-form update from a target customer or referral base. Most professionals give a lot of attention on LinkedIn, and you can quickly and efficiently endear yourself to your audience by taking a few minutes to engage.

Long-Form Content

Think of your long-form content on LinkedIn in a similar way that you think about your blog. In fact, in an ideal world, you have a blog that lives in each of the three media categories. Your owned media blog lives on your website. Your earned media blog lives on a targeted media platform like *Forbes*, *Psychology Today*, or *HuffPost*, for example. Your rented media blog is your long-form content on LinkedIn. If you don't have a blog currently on either owned or earned media, the good news is that you can start with a rented media blog on LinkedIn without spending a dime.

Let's start with the best news for those of you who are shaking your head and feeling overwhelmed at the thought of adding another blog to your to-do list—you can cut and paste blogs that you write for your owned and earned media blogs and paste them to LinkedIn as native content.

Normally we don't want you duplicating content because it's a negative for search engine optimization, but you can do so on LinkedIn because, as we write this, Google does not crawl long-form content on LinkedIn—only static profile content. When you take a column that you published on Forbes.com and share the link over to LinkedIn as a short-form update, you're going to get only marginal views because LinkedIn's algorithm isn't going to show the link to many people, again because it directs them to someone else's real estate. Instead, publish the article as native content on LinkedIn by clicking the "write an article" prompt and pasting in your content. At the top and bottom of your post, you can mention that "this article originally appeared on Forbes.com" as a way to both credit Forbes (or wherever the blog appears) and get the authority by association you want from the post.

For long-form content on LinkedIn, we want you to follow the same three global content categories that umbrella all of your content (as discussed in chapter 8):

- You-Driven content

- News-Driven content

- Relationship-Driven content

When you publish long-form content on LinkedIn, make sure you tag it with the most accurate hashtags to give it the best opportunity for discoverability beyond your connections and followers. If appropriate, share it within groups that will benefit from reading it as well, since this can lead to more views and followers.

Often the most effective form for long-form content on LinkedIn is their newsletter feature, which is available to you once you shift your profile to Creator Mode. A LinkedIn newsletter has a huge upside for leaders reading this book because of the engagement a good one creates with your audience.

If you can't tell by now, we're huge fans of LinkedIn, especially in its current form. Sure, it's still a great place to find talent for open positions, but the larger value in today's media landscape is the ability to efficiently build and nurture relationships with those who can help you grow your business. Success on LinkedIn is a combination of smart and intentional branding (static profile) and consistent, quality content across both short and long form. If you follow the blueprint we laid out above, we are confident it will become one of your favorite platforms as well. Just don't forget that as much as we all like it, it's still rented media, and LinkedIn is the equivalent of your landlord.

WHERE DOES ADVERTISING FIT?

Advertising in today's landscape shows up in many different forms, from social media ads to traditional print spreads. The one thing that remains the same is the reality that it provides the lowest level of authority possible for a rented media message. After all, your audience knows that anyone with a budget can buy an ad, so it does little to create your Authority Advantage unless you integrate it with earned and owned media.

While there are plenty of people who blow advertising budgets on the wrong media outlets or poor targeting, the vast majority of advertising waste comes from ads that try to convert a cold prospect to buying immediately. Instead, think of advertising as a great way to generate awareness and drive cold prospects to some way they can engage with you or your brand without spending money (i.e., a great lead magnet like a quiz or whitepaper).

This goes back to the most expensive awareness trap that we wholeheartedly want you to avoid. If you are spending a *dime* on advertising that is focused on a Hail Mary completion (driving someone who doesn't know you toward a purchase or no-purchase decision), put the brakes on that strategy immediately. Additionally, if you are spending money on advertising that is driving your audience back to corporate assets, you have a lower chance of converting that click into action.

Even though there are plenty of things to avoid, this doesn't mean advertising—when targeted correctly—isn't a great way to create awareness. The problem today is how to target effectively.

Recent mobile software updates—led by Apple—have been a strong response to growing momentum to shore up privacy and consumer rights on mobile devices.

The company's iOS 14 software update series dealt perhaps the biggest blow to advertisers with its change in how it managed the identifier for advertisers (IDFA). IDFA is a unique ID assigned to each iOS device, which allows app publishers to track activity on a specific device as it moves between apps and websites, with the aim of providing more individualized and targeted advertising.

In previous versions of iOS, users could opt-out by choosing the "limit ad tracking" option in their device settings. This resulted in roughly 30 percent of users opting out in 2020, according to Motley Fool.[5]

But as part of its iOS 14 software updates, devices started notifying iPhone users of the tracking and specifically require users to opt-in for each app in order to continue being tracked. As a result of Apple requiring device holders to specifically opt-in, 62 percent of users opted out according to a study by AppsFlyer.[6]

This update from Apple is just one example of the kind of step many platforms have taken to insulate their users from privacy concerns and, let's be honest, themselves from liability. It also cost ad-dependent platforms like Facebook billions of dollars in lost advertising revenue, because it has now become *much* more difficult to conduct targeted advertising.

Additionally, many companies who previously relied heavily on hyper-targeted advertising via rented media to drive lead flow are now left behind, because they do not own the connection to their audience (and now are prevented from reaching them effectively with ads). This is one of many reasons we whole-heartedly advocate for owning both your data and your audience.

---

5   Danny Vena, "Apple's Latest Privacy Move Is a Blow for Facebook, but Not The Trade Desk. Here's Why," Motley Fool, January 4, 2021, https://www.fool.com/investing/2021/01/04/apple-privacy-drops-bomb-facebook-trade-desk/.

6   AppsFlyer, "The Impact of iOS 14+ and ATT on the Mobile App Economy," last updated December 21, 2021, https://www.appsflyer.com/resources/reports/ios-14-att-dashboard/.

Yet despite all of these setbacks, advertising still has a key role as a rented media strategy for many companies because it's the one thing that you can press the accelerator on at-will once you find an approach that is delivering results.

Perhaps the biggest positive of advertising is that it positions you to generate as many impressions as your budget allows and is the best way to provide awareness to a call to action (lead magnet) that is working well. Some experienced digital marketers see the intersection of advertising with a lead magnet that is delivering as an ATM machine. For X amount of spend, the funnel delivers Y amount of ROI, and that is the holy grail of marketing funnels.

The biggest knock on advertising as it relates to creating an Authority Advantage is that it provides the lowest amount of authority, because anyone that can fog up a glass and has a budget can buy it. As a result, it becomes incredibly important to integrate your earned media into your advertising spend. If space allows, build authority within the ad itself. If you're buying ads within social media and have a short character limit, understand that you'll need to be very compelling with a clear call to action on your landing page for your lead magnet to generate results.

The success of your advertising efforts is ultimately dependent on an equation that has three parts:

- **TARGETING:** Did you hit the right media outlet that gets to the right audience?

- **LEAD MAGNET:** Did you make the right offer in your ad?

- **BUDGET MANAGEMENT:** Remember that your advertising campaign is limited to outlets that provide you with the potential for ROI.

If you miss on any of these three, you're not going to get the results you want from the money you are spending on advertising. In general, our experience has shown that advertising is a better tool to use once everything else is working really well. It's a way to pour gas on the fire once you have established your Authority Advantage rather than the best way to spark initial interest.

11

EARNED MEDIA

TRUE TO ITS NAME, earned media includes all content that goes out on real estate others own where the impression of the audience is that you *earned* that message. It includes:

- Publicity

- Speaking engagements

- Online business or book reviews

- Referrals

- Word of mouth

- Awards

To be clear, earned media can be positive or negative depending on the message being communicated. But assuming it *is* positive, nothing provides more immediate authority than earned media. As a result, many would-be authorities make the mistake of putting all their eggs in this single basket.

This is one of the most limiting traps to fall into. When you rely solely or primarily on earned media for exposure and lead flow, you limit your reach and leverage because you don't have any direct control over the message going out.

Instead, in the earned media category, you only have indirect control.

But the limiting factor of earned media is also the thing that gives it the most authority: it matters much more what someone else says about you rather than what you say about yourself. Therefore, we want it to be a major part of how you create your Authority Advantage.

With those caveats in place, let's look at the three most important categories of "earned media" beyond referral marketing—publicity, speaking, and publishing a book—and how to use them to create your Authority Advantage.

THE MAGIC OF GOOD PUBLICITY

For most experts, PR and media are the crown jewels of the earned media category, and for good reason. Having your name in print in the *New York Times* or on a banner across the bottom of a CNBC screen is the kind of splashy media appearance that can be leveraged throughout the course of one's career. Listen to the next few speaker introductions you hear at conferences, and you'll notice how many of them include lines like "Has been quoted by …" or "Featured in …"

That kind of authority by association accelerates trust in a way that few other pillars of authority marketing can.

Almost irrationally, we assign buckets and buckets of authority to someone who has been featured in *Forbes* or interviewed on FOX News, which is why PR and media is such an important part of your authority blueprint.

The magic in such appearances isn't the huge audience you reach—although that's nice, assuming the interview goes well. Rather, it's the ability to remarket that interview and the associated media logo from that point forward to build your authority.

There are essentially three different levels of value on the publicity front:

1. The first level is the audience you reach. If you're doing a live TV or radio interview or you've gotten an article published, the most obvious and direct piece of value is the audience that will take in your content. They hear you speak or read your article, and that may motivate them to hire you for a speech or buy a book from you. That's what most people are concerned with when it comes to PR and media. They want to sell something or promote their services or products to that audience.

2. The second level of value, which is actually much more important in terms of building lasting authority, is the ability to remarket that media coverage. When you have an article in *Forbes*, for example, that logo can go on your website and in your marketing materials for the rest of your career. That mention of *Forbes* becomes part of the way you're introduced on TV or at speaking engagements. The remarketing of media coverage and the authority by association that comes with being featured on major media outlets is one of the most

important pieces of value that comes from publicity. If you're reading this book and you have not done media, then you don't have media brand logos to showcase. You should know that is one of the most important levers you can pull to quickly ramp up your authority.

3. The third level of value in publicity is also very important. It goes back to an idea we have talked about in this book— the idea of not just entertaining and engaging audiences but actually giving people a reason to head to your stadium via the lead magnet you offer. In other words, you're using that interview or article to drive people back to your owned media and grow your email list. That's why it is so important to have the right lead magnet in place, so you really maximize your value from any publicity. Without that, you will only be benefiting from a fraction of the value you could be getting from publicity opportunities.

Being interviewed regularly creates a sense of "omnipresence" while positively building your brand, which is one reason you don't want to build a flash-in-the-pan approach to PR. Instead, you want to set up a strategy that creates sustained momentum over time.

That's the good news.

The more challenging news for all who want to generate meaningful publicity is that the game has changed dramatically when it comes to actually landing it. Thanks to shuttered print outlets and consolidated TV and radio production, today's environment has fewer major mass media outlets, even while micromedia is more plentiful than ever before.

In today's new media landscape, there are fewer and fewer journalists at traditional media outlets, and those who remain are now tasked with more work than ever. They must fill up the newspapers, websites, and social media channels with good content. As such, you have more and more marketers pitching fewer and fewer journalists. We talk with media members who get upward of a thousand pitches a day, making this traditional push process extremely difficult, but not impossible.

The most effective way to get PR today is to have a push/pull approach, where you pitch ideas directly to the media while also pulling them to you via smart content marketing. We're going to organize most of this chapter around helping you integrate these two approaches.

PUSH

This is the "traditional" process that you likely think about when it comes to garnering publicity. This process begins with creating a strategy, crafting a press kit, and pitching media outlets story ideas in the hope of grabbing their attention. While this process still works today, it's less reliable and more dependent on having a publicist who truly has solid media relationships in place.

For most leaders, there are three media groups that make the most sense to target as part of a publicity campaign.

Name-Brand Traditional Media

This category includes traditional media that have been on wish lists for entrepreneurs and leaders for decades and decades, from the *New York Times* to CNBC to *Forbes* and beyond. If you want to be viewed as an authority, one of the quickest ways to facilitate that is to associate yourself with brands that have more built-in authority with your audience than almost anything else besides a book.

The main value with this category of media is the ability to remarket it for years to drive people to your website and beyond as compared to the lead flow you get from other categories.

It is important to understand that media reps on this level are not looking for reasons to book you. They are looking for reasons *not* to book you. If your publicist is fortunate enough to capture their attention, the next step for most producers, editors, and journalists is to do their due diligence with both Google and YouTube searches. They are looking for red flags that would prevent a booking, including (but not limited to) bad customer reviews, an amateurish website, confusing messaging/branding, or anything else that would make them question whether or not you are the authority in your topic area. This is another reason that you must both a) own search around your name, and b) ensure the image you create in the minds of those searching positions you as the authority. We see many people jump right to hiring a publicist without having their brand in shape and their publicist ends up fighting an uphill battle—because even interested journalists end up getting turned off by amateurish content and branding.

EXTRA TIP FOR GARNERING NAME-BRAND MEDIA: Add a press room to your website. Your press room should include four sections:

- **CONTACT INFORMATION FOR YOUR PUBLICIST:** Make it as easy as possible for a journalist to get in touch with you.

- **LINKS TO RECENT MEDIA COVERAGE:** When a journalist lands on your press room and sees you have done a lot of other media interviews, it tells them that someone else has already vetted you and often accelerates their willingness to reach out.

- **DOWNLOADABLE LINKS:** Have your headshot, press kit, and a high-res book cover available for download.

- **A LIST OF SUGGESTED QUESTIONS** the interviewer can refer to.

Micromedia

While name-brand media provides much more credibility than micromedia, the reality is that well-targeted micromedia will almost always produce significantly more lead flow. As a reminder, micromedia includes podcasts, blogs, newsletters, webinars, and beyond that are run by smaller, hypertargeted individuals and organizations.

We recently had a *New York Times* best-selling author whom we have worked with on several book launches come back to us for her most recent one. She expressed that the only thing she wanted us to pursue was this category of media. Despite her previous campaign, which included a national morning show and several top print hits, her data showed that the vast majority of the actual purchases, from her book to her e-learning program to her speaking engagements, came from podcasts, blogs, and newsletters.

This plays into broader trends in the media landscape that we are seeing—trust in "legacy" media is eroding while trust in micromedia is through the roof.

> **TRUST IN "LEGACY" MEDIA IS ERODING WHILE TRUST IN MICROMEDIA IS THROUGH THE ROOF.**

Thus, when a podcaster, blogger, or other individual outlet recommends you and your book, their audience often jumps to act in a much different way than the audience of large, generic media.

EXTRA TIP FOR GARNERING MICROMEDIA COVERAGE: One of the best ways to build relationships with top podcasters is to avoid beginning the relationship by asking for something. Instead, start by inviting them onto your podcast or to do a Q and A with you on your blog. The micromedia space runs largely on the law of reciprocation, and you'll be amazed at how many of the people you feature will turn around and invite you onto their platform as well.

Local Media

The last media category that we want you to include in your target list is local media. Even though you may not sell primarily in your local market, local coverage is not only rewarding for most but also good for your personal network to "see" you in action within media they follow routinely.

Depending on the size of your local market, sometimes the fact that you are releasing a book will be enough to generate media coverage. If you live in a larger city, you may need to create a local event (like a book signing) that is open to the public as a hook to get their attention. Often, they simply need a reason to cover you right now, and an event can provide that reason (they typically won't cover a private event).

EXTRA TIP FOR LOCAL MEDIA: Follow local on-air and print personalities on Twitter, and find ways to engage with them that don't involve asking for anything. Over time, you'll build relationships that lead to inbound opportunities.

PULL

When you are pushing pitches at the media, it's always going to be harder to generate exposure—because you're trying to talk them into covering a story that you want covered, not that they necessarily want to cover. On the flip side, when you pull the media to you, you fit yourself into a story they already know they want to cover, and often it leads to the biggest media coverage you'll get.

In today's landscape, we often say that Google can be a great publicist, and that's because when a journalist decides they want to cover a certain story, many of them head to Google or Twitter in search of more information and often potential sources.

It's certainly not easy to get a call from CNBC, but there are a number of things you can do to increase your likelihood of catching a journalist's attention, beginning with these action items:

- **SIGN UP FOR INBOUND MEDIA REQUEST SERVICES**

    One of the best innovations in the PR space in the past ten years was created by an entrepreneur by the name of Peter Shankman. Shankman recognized how inefficient the traditional "push" process is for journalists and decided to flip it around—instead of PR reps and experts guessing what the media wants to cover, he launched Help a Reporter Out (HARO), which is a daily email that goes out with live media queries. Since the launch of HARO, many more similar services have been launched, including great new ones like Qwoted, but the utility is just the same—the emails are full of queries from pro journalists requesting to speak with specific types of experts for stories they are working on. It's the one time a journalist will say, "I'm looking for an expert on plastic surgery for burn victims. If you are one, please pitch me." We have seen many leaders self-generate significant PR attention through these services.

- **PUSH OUT TIMELY CONTENT**

    We discussed earlier how content that's more tied into the current news is much more potent than evergreen content. PR is another reason News-Driven content is such a vital tool. It allows you to widen your net around certain topics, as statistics show that journalists are increasingly turning to Google, Twitter, Help A Reporter, News & Experts, and other online resources when they need an expert to speak on a breaking news topic. When you have created a "newsjacking" post, you widen your net to attract media to you rather than trying to stand out among a thousand daily pitches. It also facilitates relationship building with media personalities. Media members are more frequently looking to build these kinds of relationships with authorities.

- **MAKE IT EASY FOR THE MEDIA**

  As mentioned earlier in this book, you must make it easy for the media to reach out to you. If you have a website, make sure you have a press room. If you don't have a press room, understand which pages come up in a search on your name. For many experts, this is a bio page on their organization's website. Make sure there is current contact information on that page. If you don't make it easy for them to reach you, they're going to move on to the next expert.

- **DON'T LET YOUR SOCIAL MEDIA INFRASTRUCTURE LANGUISH**

  Few things look worse to media members or readers than a social media extension that hasn't been updated in months. Don't set up a Facebook page or Twitter account unless you intend to engage there and provide consistent, valuable content. If you have social media accounts that you don't update, cancel the accounts.

- **HAVE AN OPINION**

  This should be a given, right? Surprisingly, no. Many experts stay in the middle of the road, which doesn't really drive interest or sharing on either side of a debate. Your odds of getting your content in front of a journalist within social media are boosted dramatically if you are writing provocative pieces that your readers want to share with their networks. This doesn't mean to get super controversial, but people don't engage with those who stand for nothing—so be interesting, and have a take.

Now, let's answer a couple more common questions about PR.

Do I Need to Hire a Publicist, and How Do I Do That?

The good news is that in today's landscape, hiring a publicist isn't your only route to generating good PR, as we detailed earlier in the "Pull" section of the PR strategy. With that said, good publicists provide three things for you:

1. **MEDIA RELATIONSHIPS:** Good publicists are a filter for the media, which is why their calls are taken and their emails are opened at a much higher rate.

2. **TIME TO FOCUS ON THE RIGHT OPPORTUNITIES:** If you don't have time, or if your time is far too valuable to spend on the pull strategies mentioned above, a publicist can take this off your plate.

3. **UNDERSTANDING WHICH OPPORTUNITIES TO PURSUE:** In the age of micromedia, where every individual and company can launch a podcast at any time, knowledge of which ones are valuable and which ones aren't is a huge boost. A publicist can help you determine which are worth focusing on.

While good publicists do bring a lot to the table, there are plenty of bad ones out there who charge a lot of money to generate zero results. But whether you are hiring Forbes Books or another publicity firm, here are a few things to ensure before you sign a deal:

❏ **DID THEY VET YOU?** A good publicist is going to interview you as much as you interview them. If a publicist is putting a proposal in front of you before taking a deep dive into your background, goals, and messaging, you are probably dealing with a questionable one.

❏ **CAN THEY DEMONSTRATE RESULTS IN YOUR VERTICAL?** Most publicists have long lists of name-brand media they can show you, but a good litmus test is whether or not they have booked high-value micromedia in your vertical. What podcasts, blogs, newsletters, and other opportunities that you actually consume (and know your clients consume) have they booked with?

❏ **ARE THEY ON THE HOOK FOR RESULTS?** In other words, is there any way to keep them accountable for results in your campaign?

What's the ROI of PR and Media?

A final point on PR and media is that in today's world it has become easy to track your audience. In the past, people would have to ask, "What's the ROI? How do I know for sure that your interview led to me getting clients?"

That's always been a tough question for PR firms to handle. But now, thanks to data mining and analytics, you have the ability to track which people are interacting with which content online. Who are the people actually engaging with your article through "likes" and comments? Who shared it? Who's tweeting about it? How many people came to your website from the article? Build systems to help you track results—although it can be hard to attribute specific leads to specific media interviews, it's not unheard of with the right funnel in place.

But, as described earlier in this section, the most important value that comes from PR and media is not the immediacy of lead flow—it's the ability to associate yourself and your business with the halo of authority that comes from those outlets that do cover you. A good publicist can make the right media connections happen for you.

LEVERAGING SPEAKING TO CREATE YOUR AUTHORITY ADVANTAGE

Few things make you feel like more of an authority than thunderous applause at the end of a well-delivered keynote.

Yet, as good as that feeling of accomplishment is, perhaps the more important impact will happen in the following hours, days, and weeks as the audience members are converted to customers, referral bases, and fans.

If PR and media are perceived as the crown jewels of authority in the minds of most experts (besides publishing a book), keynote speaking isn't far behind. Speaking can create significant income streams through fees alone, but the opportunity to sell products at the back of the room, generate leads and interest from the audience, and co-opt other people's customers to become your customers make speaking one of the most desired and sought after of earned media categories.

Patti Brennan puts it like this:

When people see me on a stage, for example, even if it's a still picture, the subliminal message that they're getting is, "Hey, Patti's considered a thought leader. She's up on a stage. I wonder what she thinks about my situation."

That authority, that nonverbal subliminal message is "This person clearly knows what they're talking about." They have credibility—they're not trying to sell me something.

It's an interesting dichotomy—public speaking is the American public's biggest phobia, and yet it is unquestionably among the most sought-after skills for business leaders.

But as you'll read in this section, while delivering on stage may be the most important component of building a successful speaking platform, it's just one of three steps you'll need to focus on to win as a speaker. Those three steps include the following:

1. Branding

2. Delivering on stage

3. Capitalizing on each engagement

We're going to dive into detail on each of these steps, and we want to encourage you to be honest with yourself on which area needs the most immediate attention from you as you continue on your authority-building journey.

STEP 1: BUILDING YOUR BRAND AS A SPEAKER

When you think of keynote speakers with great brands, who comes to mind? Your list might include the likes of Tony Robbins, Sally Hogshead, and John Maxwell, among others. Each of them is an exceptionally gifted orator who accelerated their growth through creating an Authority Advantage. Our goal for those of you who want to speak more is to begin down the same road.

There are a lot of successful businesspeople who want to do more speaking and are puzzled as to why they're not getting more opportunities. In many cases, it's not that they can't deliver on stage (though in some cases it is); it's that they're not well positioned online as a speaker. Instead, they're positioned as a financial planner, attorney, or business owner—someone any meeting planner will see more as a vendor or potential sponsor than a speaker.

It all comes back to branding.

This is a key reason we encourage people to plant a flag for themselves as an authority with a standalone website, as that is a place where you can be featured as a mission-driven thought leader, author, speaker, and media personality. It connotes a whole different brand than a corporate website that lists you as CEO, especially if you're wanting to speak.

If we are planning an event, and you pitch us to speak at the event with a link to your bio on your corporate website, we are going to forward your pitch to our sponsorship chair to see if we can sell you a booth (and lunch and learn) at the conference.

But if we get a link to a speaking page on a standalone website where you're a published author, and we see a photo of you giving a keynote speech, perhaps even find a video of you giving speeches, our perception shifts. Now we are wondering how much of our budget we need to set aside to get you to our event as we sweat whether or not you're going to ask for first-class accommodations in addition to your speaking fee.

The second phase of branding yourself as a speaker involves the assets you have in place.

First, you need a speaker's kit within your website. Ideally, we want you to lean into visuals on stage and to leverage books.

The goal of this kit is not to have a client land on a specific keynote topic (that should happen during a prep call with you and/or their speaker's bureau) but instead to demonstrate with as little doubt as possible in the minds of the kit's viewer that you have delivered keynotes with rave reviews on some of the biggest stages in the world. This is incredibly important because the biggest fear in the minds of those considering booking you for a speech is that you won't be able to deliver in front of a large audience. The more you can do to lower that fear, the more likely you are to get the gig.

Ideally you want the following items in your speaker's kit:

- A speaker-focused bio

- Logos from past events and media appearances

- Three to five popular keynote topics you can speak to

- Quotes from people who have heard you speak

- Specific names of conferences where you have spoken (omit this if you are just getting started)

Secondly, you need a promotional speaker's reel. This is a highlight video (often called a "sizzle reel") that is typically two to four minutes long and provides highlights from several different speeches. This should be a video that combines quick stage clips with as much authority by association as possible in the form of logos, endorsements, and other trust-building visuals.

The third key asset you must have is a raw ten-to-twenty-minute unedited video of you on stage giving a speech. This is being requested more and more frequently by event planners because it really shows that you can deliver on stage without the help of flashy graphics or fast-paced editing. What tends to really sell them is not something they know is edited within an inch of its life to make you look as good as possible. Rather, it's the unedited twenty-minute video that opens your speaking kimono in terms of whether or not you really can deliver. They may sell you to their board or the powers that be with your speaker kit and highlight reel—but only if convinced to do so by your raw video.

These three assets are the best starting points for business leaders who want to position themselves with a brand as a speaker.

Now that you know how to position yourself to do more speaking, let's look at two of the most common questions we get from leaders: "Do I speak for free or charge a fee?" and "Where should I speak?"

Most people start speaking for free. This allows them to gain experience and develop those visual assets we just discussed. It affords an opportunity to get video and pictures of themselves speaking. It also brings in other speaking opportunities. In the beginning, most speaking opportunities come from people who were sitting in the audience of a previous speech. In other words, giving a speech for free excites people and translates into additional speaking engagements.

The more a person speaks, the higher their authority rises, thus affording the ability to call more shots about where they speak and what the context is. Once a speaker has established authority, they can start charging a speaking fee. However, there will be certain conferences where the audience is of such high quality—where you can derive incredible value from being on stage—that it may be best to waive a speaking fee. This is especially true if the audience is composed of potential customers.

Imagine yourself in such a position. If you know you can generate $50,000 out of that audience if a few of them become customers of your business, then it may be worth speaking for free rather than charging a fee. But first you must get to a point in your career where those decisions are your own and not someone else's.

Now, back to the question of where you should speak.

Speaking engagements are either in person or virtual. In-person events within your local market are easy to do. If they're outside your local market, that requires a commitment that likely involves the friendly skies. The events that are going to provide the biggest value to you are those most concentrated in your highest-value lead bases. These may not be the most popular or glamorous conferences. They might not have the largest social media shares. However, if the right twenty to fifty people are in the room, that makes all the difference. Even if you get just a small group from the niche audiences you want to target, that can be much more powerful and beneficial to you than speaking to a thousand people who are not your customers. Remember, the riches are in the niches.

REMEMBER, THE RICHES ARE IN THE NICHES.

With in-person events, it's important to consider the amount of time it is going to take you. Then, weigh that against the likelihood that you're going to get a significant return on your investment of time and resources. If you do decide to attend a large in-person event, there is one thing you absolutely must be sure to do—get professional photos! If you speak at a big event—especially where there is a great backdrop—and you don't get professional photos, you are missing a massive opportunity. Don't just have your family snap some shots with their phones; spend $500 and hire a professional photographer. These types of photos can be immensely valuable for your website and speaking packages.

Another key thing to remember is that most speaking engagements live in the earned media category. As such, we encourage you to keep the same one-two punch mindset in place. The first area of focus is delivering great content—obviously, you need to crush it on stage—but the second area of focus is siphoning off as much of this audience as possible and driving them back to your stadium.

STEP 2: DELIVERING ON STAGE

Step 2 takes us right back to America's biggest phobia: the actual speaking-in-public part. It's important to remember that all speakers—even the most dynamic main-stage keynote icons—all started out scared out of their minds.

Though neither of us would count ourselves in the category of top speakers we listed early in this section, I (Rusty) can certainly relate to the "scared out of my mind" part, especially for one particularly intimidating stage.

I was twenty-three years old and working as a publicist in Austin, Texas, when an email hit my inbox from another member of our team, Steve Morse. Steve had been pitching a health journal in the Boston area, and the physician editor on the other end of the line of that particular phone pitch said she was putting on a CME (continuing medical education) conference on publishing for Harvard Medical School and needed a good book publicist to give the PR talk.

She had worked with us a few times and asked if anyone at the firm would be a good fit. After getting her contact info, Steve sent an email around the office asking if anyone wanted to reach out to her about speaking at the event.

Without thinking about the implications, I picked up the phone and called Dr. Silver. I told her I would be happy to fly to Boston to give the speech and could bring some fresh ideas to the table (left unsaid was that I wouldn't be bringing a lot of speaking experience). Knowing it would be an issue when I arrived, I also let her know that I was young but knew my stuff. Although I was twenty-three, I looked like I was fourteen years old—and I was praying she didn't ask me my age because I knew the opportunity would probably be dead in the water. Thankfully, she didn't, and we had a great conversation that led to me heading to Boston as a faculty member at the course in 2005.

A few months later, I walked into the banquet room at the Fairmont Copley in Boston the night before the big speech. After getting my name tag from the registration table, I walked up to

Dr. Silver to introduce myself. She turned from the person she was speaking with, and I said, "Hi, I'm Rusty Shelton—it's great to meet you." She looked like she had seen a ghost. "Wow! You are *way* younger than I expected." I know she was beyond nervous when I hit the stage the next day for my speech—we both were. I remember feeling like I was going to faint as she handed me the mic after introducing me. Thankfully, a piece of wisdom that had been shared with me in college was confirmed to me that day: the only thing that trumps nerves is preparation. I had given that speech to the wall in my office every day for a month straight, and fortunately muscle memory kicked in and I delivered one of the most important speeches of my life.

Practice is incredibly important, but it's certainly just the starting point when it comes to delivering on stage, as we have learned over the course of giving hundreds of speeches around the world. Here are our four biggest recommendations:

1.) *Win the first two minutes.*

Speeches are won or lost in the first two minutes on stage. If you win the opening, you have the audience's attention for the remainder of your time on stage. If you lose them early, no matter how good the rest of your speech is, they have already mentally checked out.

SPEECHES ARE WON OR LOST IN THE FIRST TWO MINUTES ON STAGE.

SOLUTION: Open every speech with an attention grabber that you can deliver in your sleep. The ideal opening is either a) an emotionally powerful or funny narrative, or b) a counterintuitive or surprising situational analysis that snatches their attention.

2.) *Never call attention to a mistake on stage.*

This is a mistake we both made quite a bit early in our careers. If a slide deck wasn't working, if we happened to insert an incorrect hashtag in a slide, or if we had a cough, we'd feel compelled to mention it as a nod to what we projected as the audience's awareness of it.

Amateur hour.

Your job as a keynote speaker is to deliver awesome content that creates value for the audience, and any mistake a speaker calls attention to (no matter how much it may be bothering that speaker) diverts the audience's attention to that issue and away from their content. As we mentioned, we often made this mistake early in our careers and continue to see too many speakers do it. Here are a few things we've heard some of them say recently:

- "Sorry—for whatever reason, I have some nerves this morning."

- "I have to apologize—since the speaker in front of me went long, I'm going to have to go extra fast."

- "That's quite a cough there in the front row—you need some water?"

- "Wow, this feels like an interrogation—that spotlight is right in my eyes. Can someone turn that thing down?"

- "We tested the AV just this morning—not sure what happened to the slide deck! So frustrating."

- "Wow, is anyone else hot in here?"

SOLUTION: Each of the issues above is your problem as the speaker—not the audience's. In most cases, they will never know there's an issue unless you call attention to it. When you do that, you essentially ask them to focus on that issue instead of your content, and when that happens, everyone loses. Power through at all times with confidence and grit.

3.) *Watch every speech of yours you possibly can on video after the engagement.*

Sitting down to watch yourself speak sounds a bit egotistical, right? I (Rusty) certainly thought so early in my career and went out of my way to deliver what I thought was great content and then move on to the next talk.

The first speech of mine that I saw on camera was a talk to the Writers League of Texas when I was about twenty-five. It was a monthly education event, and the local access TV station here in Austin decided to come out and film it. My big break! I gave what I thought was a great speech, and two weeks later my wife, Paige, and I sat down on the couch to watch it on a Wednesday night at nine o'clock. I'll never forget the embarrassment I felt as I spent forty-five minutes with my hand over my mouth completely horrified at what I was watching. Paige, by comparison, was having a good laugh at my expense.

On stage during the speech, I was doing something subconsciously. For some reason, every time I would make a point, I would press down my right hand—fingers fully outstretched—like I was hitting piano keys. I looked like the piano man up there. I must have done it a hundred times during a forty-five-minute speech, and I'm sure the audience was losing their minds wondering what the hell I was doing.

I wasn't consciously doing it, but that tic caused the audience to be totally distracted from my message (and probably a bit amused). The only way to ferret out that kind of tick is to watch yourself in a stressful environment and observe what you may be doing.

SOLUTION: Videotape every speech you can (even if just an iPhone video—these aren't for distribution) and review them back to look for nonverbal tics like my Billy Joel impersonation, or words you're saying too much ("Right?").

4.) *Relentlessly focus on audience value.*

Speaking isn't about you—it's about making an impact on the audience you're speaking to. The more confident you are, the more attention they'll pay. The more personalized your examples, narratives, and statistics are, the more relevant the content will be. The humbler and more vulnerable you are with your narratives, the more willing the audience will be to let down their guard and listen to your insight.

SOLUTION: Although there are a thousand things that go into being a great speaker, when you focus on audience value, everything else tends to fall into place because you are putting yourself more at ease. Instead of focusing on you and how you look or sound on stage, you focus on delivering value, and as a result, you look and sound better.

The good news is that every speech you do is an audition for five, ten, or twenty more based on word of mouth from those in the audience, so follow the above advice and give them every reason to go back to their group, association, or conference and recommend you as the most dynamic speaker they've heard this year.

STEP 3: CAPITALIZE ON EVERY ENGAGEMENT

We touched earlier in this section on the importance of having crystal clarity on your desired outcome surrounding each speaking engagement you do.

If you are being paid a fee to speak, your primary goal is to overdeliver with your content; follow-up sales become the gravy on top. If you are speaking to sell (no fee up front), your primary goal is still to overdeliver with your content, but the arc of your speech needs to change a bit to ensure you drive that audience toward an outcome where you can serve them further through more products and services.

A consistent goal across both types of speeches is the need to extend your interaction with the audience via a high-quality lead magnet. There are two ways to leverage a lead magnet in conjunction with a speaking engagement.

The first and most obvious is to use it as a call to action at the end of the speech. If you're the authors of *The Confidence Code* and have just spent an hour speaking to the women's leadership conference at Morgan Stanley, you might close your speech with a slide that highlights, say, a free confidence assessment available on your website (this is a tactic we'll discuss in further detail in the next chapter on owned media).

"We're sure that after hearing this talk, many of you may be wondering where you fall on the confidence spectrum. We get that question so much we set up a free assessment that has been taken by more than two hundred thousand people over the past three years. Go to our website to see where you stand."

This kind of call to action works tremendously well at a paid speaking engagement because it doesn't have an ounce of sales focus and allows you to extend your interaction with the audience in an elegant way that provides them with all the value.

The second and perhaps even better way to do it is to get that kind of assessment link to the audience *before* you walk on stage. As many of you might guess, meeting planners are always very vigilant about not providing email addresses for attendees to speakers to shield them from unwanted marketing messages. Of course, we want you to have as many of those email addresses as possible, and the best way to accomplish that is to create a win-win for both you and the meeting planner.

Do this by highlighting the fact that you use your assessment tool to personalize your speaking engagement. Sally Hogshead is a master at this. She has the meeting planner send out a link for the audience to take her "Fascination Advantage Assessment" ahead of her speaking engagement. She normally charges for this assessment but can also include it in the fee for a speaking engagement. The audience takes it ahead of time—which is a win for them because they are getting free results for something they would otherwise have to pay for. Then, when Sally hits the stage, her first few slides reflect back the data of the audience. This positions her as a data-driven, hyperpersonalized speaker, which is exactly what most meeting planners are looking for. At the same time, it gives her a way to serve the audience further by personalizing a follow-up sequence for them based on their results.

Again, most meeting planners won't be willing to give you an email list of the audience, but if you package your request in a way that gives huge value to your presentation, they will indirectly give you access to that list. In addition to delivering a more personalized speech thanks to the data from the audience, you have also just added a lot of fans of your brand.

Here is how Verne Harnish makes the most of each of his speaking engagements:

> We include 500 books with every speaking gig, which provides both exposure from stage and something they can take with them afterward to read if they found the presentation useful. In addition, our 200+ coaching partners host regular one-day workshops that further introduce potential clients to the power of our approach to scaling without all the drama normally associated with growing a firm.

Both of us enjoy speaking as much or more than just about any other earned media strategy. It's fun, rewarding, and drives more audience engagement and impact than anything besides a book.

At the same time, it's a long journey to build steady, predictable income from speaking engagements. Don't put too much pressure on yourself early regarding the size of the audiences you're speaking to or the amount of money you're generating via speaking fees. Instead, use each opportunity as a chance to get pictures and videos, and begin generating referrals. Over time, as you blend speaking for fees with speaking to sell, we're confident it will become an incredibly important part of building your Authority Advantage.

IT'S HARD TO SPELL AUTHORITY WITHOUT *AUTHOR*

The first six letters of the word *authority* tell us something about the word's relationship to writing and publishing a book. For whatever reasons, right or wrong, people look at authors of books as authorities.

An analogy we like to use involves runners. The ultimate achievement in running is to complete a marathon. Lots of people run, and they might knock off a mile or two a few times a week. They race through their neighborhood, and after those couple of miles or so, they're feeling pretty good, but they're beat. To most people the thought of running 26.2 miles seems impossible. That's why when we meet someone who has run a marathon, we're automatically impressed.

Writing and publishing a book is the same thing. You may write every day—many people do, whether it be emails, journals, or even business-related content. But writing anything more than a thousand words feels like a marathon for most. The thought of writing forty thousand to fifty thousand words seems as impossible as running 26.2 miles. Writing a letter, a blog post, or a few emails is a jog in the park while writing a book is a marathon.

Because the vast majority of people have never written more than a thousand words at a time, the idea of writing an entire book is a daunting task. You might as well be asking them to scale Mount Everest. And because of the enormity of the task, there's a psychological reaction they have when you introduce yourself as an author. You instantly gain a significant amount of respect because you have accomplished that feat. Most people don't even need to know what your book is about or have read it. Respect is earned as soon as they hear you say, "I am the author of ..."

That's why writing a book can be a foundational element of creating your Authority Advantage. It is a force multiplier. It enables you to establish instant respect and credibility with whomever you meet, and if a person takes the time to read the book, you also

WRITING A BOOK CAN BE A FOUNDATIONAL ELEMENT OF CREATING YOUR AUTHORITY ADVANTAGE. IT IS A FORCE MULTIPLIER.

have a chance to make a lasting impact on them. Publishing a book positions you as an expert on whatever topic your book is about. The perception is that if you have enough knowledge to write a book on a topic, you must know a lot more about it than most people do. We all know a little bit about a lot. But if you know enough about something to write a book on it, people assume you know enough to be *the* authority on the topic. You're seen as an expert. If you weren't an expert, how could you ever write and publish a book on that subject?

Allow us to let you in on a secret about why books are so effective as tools for creating your Authority Advantage: it's because they have never been seen as or thought of as marketing tools. Books are scholarly. Books are literary. Books are tools for educating and enlightening ourselves. Nobody thinks of books as a way to sell things, but in reality, they often are. By writing a book, you can market yourself without being seen as a self-promoter. You gain authority and expert status through a marketing tool that people do not *see* as a marketing tool, and you make a bigger impact as a result.

When you write a book, you might as well tell somebody you're a college professor. You gain a similar level of credibility through authority by association thanks to centuries and centuries of authors being looked to as authorities. Intelligence is one of the many levers that can be pulled to create authority. Albert Einstein was seen as an authority because … well, he was really smart. Stephen Hawking had a name that connotes authority because he was also viewed as one of the most intelligent people of his time. When you write a book, people immediately perceive you as someone of high intelligence—because we assume that people who write books are very bright. When you write a book, you become the teacher instead of the student.

Authority is completely psychological. When you are perceived as the teacher, that puts others in a mindset where they are ready to learn. This creates a mind shift based on trust. When you introduce yourself as an author—especially if it's a topic someone is interested in—you have a chance to make a much bigger impact because you are speaking to someone who's ready to learn. That means they are going to listen to what you have to say and will likely take your advice. This can be a total game changer, especially if you're selling something; you need people to listen to what you have to say and be willing to take your recommendations. At this point, you're prescribing solutions rather than selling products or services, and that changes everything.

Another psychological component to authoring a book is the immeasurable value society places on books. We have created permanent shrines for books—from huge libraries down to our own personal bookshelves. We proudly display our books for others to see. As such, we never throw books away. We throw away newspapers and magazines. We stream television programs and subscribe to satellite radio so we can consume the media we specifically want, disregard what we don't, and then forget about it. Essentially, all other forms of media have become disposable—but not books. Think about it. When was the last time you threw a book away? If you give us a book and we aren't interested in it, we're going to pass it along to someone who is or donate it to the library. There's a certain guilt that comes with tossing a book into the trash. As a society, humans value books and the authors who create them.

The origin of that value we place on books has Judeo-Christian roots. What's the best-selling book of all time? The Bible. The foundation of almost every organized religion as we know it is *a book*. The Muslims have the Koran, the LDS Church has the Book of Mormon, and so on.

Because many people have a religious background, whether or not they practice it today, there is an innate understanding that books are immensely important. It holds true in all cultures that a subliminal belief system exists about the value of books and the authority of those who write them.

The smartest marketers in the world are better psychologists than they are sales professionals. They understand, at its heart, that selling is about persuading and that persuading is emotional and irrational. We buy with emotion—we justify the purchase with logic after the sale.

For all these reasons, the foundational step to creating your Authority Advantage—the quickest "trust" hack that exists—is to author a book on a topic that reflects your expertise.

A book pulls all these subconscious psychological triggers and automatically earns you respect, credibility, and trust. It shifts people's mindsets and alters their perceptions of you. We've had people tell us that publishing their book even changed the way their own families looked at them! That sounds unbelievable, but it's true. Everyone has the same psychological response. We, the authors of this book, understand the psychology—and we *still* have the same response. That's why we always tell people that if you want to establish your Authority Advantage, start with authoring a book. And legendary thought leader Verne Harnish agrees with that assessment:

> We like to think the book is our "first impression" and then the website serves as a way to guide people in getting the support they need in implementing our tools and techniques. The book serves as a complete "business card"— and all our efforts are to market the book, with just over 500,000 of *Scaling Up* and 850,000 of all four books in the market—print, audio, and e-book.

Let's explore several of the most important issues involved in writing a book.

WHAT DO I WRITE ABOUT?

Before you can figure out *what* you should write about, you have to ask yourself *why* you're writing a book. There are a lot of reasons to write a book, and they're all valid in their own right.

Some people are motivated by legacy. It's a matter of them wanting to have some say in how they're remembered. "What are my grandkids and great-grandkids going to know about me? What are the employees of my company going to know about me fifty years after I am gone?" Legacy is significant, and it's a good reason to write a book. Books often cement legacy.

Education or impact is another reason. Most authorities aren't just trying to grow their business or make money. They have a true desire to make an impact by educating others and helping them make better decisions. Knowledge is power, and people are moved to share their knowledge with the world. By doing so, they can help people become more informed and have an impact on the world. Which, of course, is another excellent reason to write a book.

For some, writing a book is a bucket list item. There's nothing wrong with that. In fact, according to the *Huffington Post*, over 80 percent of Americans want to write a book before they die.[7] Only a miniscule fraction of those people actually will, but it is a widespread desire.

Many people who want to write do it to entertain others by crafting compelling stories. We all love a good story, and many works of fiction have become very influential.

However, if you're reading this book, we suspect the main reason you would want to write a book would be to grow your business and make a larger impact by creating your Authority Advantage for yourself and your company. By establishing yourself as a thought leader, you make your business and yourself a magnet for opportunity. That doesn't mean your book can't accomplish multiple goals—it can definitely educate people about what you do or the field you work in, and it can serve as a legacy builder. But along the way we want that book to open doors for you to reach a much larger group of people.

With business growth and broader impact in mind, the best advice when it comes to deciding what to write about is to bait the hook to suit the fish, not the fisherman. Many authors don't follow this simple advice. They write the book they want to write and then hope there's an audience that cares enough to read it. Instead, authors should

BAIT THE HOOK TO SUIT THE FISH, NOT THE FISHERMAN.

---

7   William Dietrich, "The Writer's Odds of Success," *Huffington Post*, last modified May 4, 2013, https://www.huffingtonpost.com/william-dietrich/the-writers-odds-of-succe_b_2806611.html.

ask, "What is the yearning, burning problem that my target customer is grappling with?" Then, when you know the answer, write a book that addresses that.

If you want to write a book that will serve as the ultimate marketing tool, you have to write about a topic that the people who have the ability and willingness to buy from you care about. If you can address the problems that your prospective customer is facing, all the better. No matter what it is, *what you write about must be of importance to people who have the capacity and ultimately the desire to give your business money*. What we mean by that is, a lot of people write a book for the masses. When you ask them who their target reader is, they'll say, "Everybody! Everybody should read my book. There's not a single person who wouldn't benefit."

The truth is, if you're writing for everybody, you're really writing for nobody. With more than 320 million people in America, and more than seven billion worldwide, there is no way your book is ever going to achieve any significant penetration in such a massive target market. As a marketer, it is financially impractical to reach a widespread global audience—you have to have a bullseye mentality when you write a book. Sure, it may benefit anyone who reads it, but if you want an efficient and effective journey to becoming an authority, you want to have a very clear idea of who will benefit most.

HOW DO I GET MY BOOK WRITTEN?

There's a reason that, even though over 80 percent of people say they want to write a book, less than a fraction of 1 percent ever do. It's not because they aren't good writers—in fact, many good writers never complete a book. It isn't because they're not passionate about it. The plain and simple fact is, writing a book takes a lot of time. Most people don't have the time to write a book, just as most people don't have the time it takes to train to run a marathon. The commitment that a task of such enormity requires is downright overwhelming—to the point where it's paralyzing for many.

There's a sign hanging at our office in Charleston, South Carolina, that reads, "How Do You Eat an Elephant?" The answer, of course, is "One bite at a time." As the ancient saying goes, the journey of a thousand miles begins with one step. The same is true of writing a book. It's just a matter of figuring out what that first step should be for you.

So how do you write your book? Well, the first answer to that question is this: Maybe you shouldn't. What we mean is, maybe you shouldn't write the book *yourself*. There's a difference between authoring a book and writing a book. Writing a book is sitting down at a computer and typing each line yourself—letting the words flow from your mind through the keyboard or onto the page. For many people, this is very, very hard.

One reason people find this so difficult is that we live incredibly distracted, fast-paced lives in a world that doesn't allow for much undivided attention. Everything today is microbursts and microseconds as opposed to long periods of uninterrupted quiet. There are mobile devices, instant news alerts, and myriad distractions that we all deal with on top of our day-to-day responsibilities.

Another reason writing a book proves difficult is that most people are better at verbalizing ideas than they are at writing them down. They can easily share their stories, passion, and knowledge verbally, but the task of writing them down and organizing them into paragraphs and chapters in a sequence that makes sense is unfamiliar and unnatural. Doing that requires a specific skill set that many people haven't learned. That's why you might want to consider working with someone who has experience doing that and can help you through the process.

Just because you may not actually be writing a book doesn't mean you aren't *authoring* it. The author of the book is the one who has the ideas and knowledge to share. A book is written in the author's voice. They are the one who ultimately decides what is included and how it is approached. A writer can help the author organize the author's ideas and get them onto the page. The author is the *authority*—a writer can be utilized to help bring the vision to life.

If you choose not to write a book yourself, there are some options. You can work with a company like ours—Forbes Books—which allows you to *talk through* your book with a professional writer. You could also hire an independent ghostwriter directly. In either scenario, you're working closely with someone who will help you turn your vision, experience, and knowledge into a book and keep you accountable along the way. We can tell you from personal experience that this is a very common method used by business professionals to create their books. It takes on average more than three years for a businessperson to write their own book. As mentioned earlier, a lot of that is due to interruptions and time constraints. By contrast, working with a third party to create your book enables you to finish the process in as little as six months.

If you do choose to write your own book—as the two of us, Adam and Rusty, each have in the past—you will have to regard it as a commitment. It is going to take discipline and regimentation. You need to begin with the end in mind. What is it going to look like? What is it going to accomplish? Who's your target reader? What problems are you addressing for them? With those questions, you should craft a blueprint for your book and then schedule time on your calendar to work on it. Block off the period of time each day that you are most productive. For some, that's early in the morning. For others, it might be the afternoon or evening. Figure out when your golden hours are—the times when you are at your best—and schedule time to write. The real trick is sticking to that schedule.

HOW DO I PUBLISH MY BOOK?

When you finally have your manuscript completed, what do you do with it? The good news is that it has never been easier to get a book published. The not-so-good news is, because it's never been easier, it's never been more important that the book be done *correctly*. Many years ago you could have cut corners, and most readers might not have noticed the difference—just having a book was itself enough to establish you as an authority. Not true anymore.

Think of it this way: If you're living in a small town, you may be the best singer there. You might have a reputation among all the locals for having a great voice. But if you were to move to Nashville or Austin, where everybody is singing at a professional level, you might discover you weren't as good as you had assumed. The same thing goes for writing a book. When nobody was publishing books, you could write a book that was a six or seven out of ten on the quality scale, and you would be okay. But now that it's become so easy to publish, you have to be a ten out of ten in quality to stand out.

Once you have your book, and you're confident it's a ten, there are three avenues you can take when it comes to publishing. You can self-publish, find a traditional publisher, or invest in independent publishing, like Forbes Books.

Self-publishing is pretty simple—you do it all yourself. That means you reap all the benefits and maintain full control of the project. That also means you have to figure everything out on your own. The big problem with self-publishing is that 90 percent of books that are self-published *look* like they're self-published. If you hear someone say, "This book looks like it was self-published," that's not a good thing. Although we're told not to judge a book by its cover, the truth is that every book's first impression is made by its cover (remember Phase One of branding—Preengagement!).

That means your book has to look as good and read as well as any you would find on the front table at Barnes & Noble or on Amazon. com. This is a must! It's not a matter of "It would be nice if it looked professional." It *has* to look the part. If your book doesn't seem every bit as good as those you find at the retail bookstores, don't publish it! If the image your book creates in the minds of your audience is not congruent with the quality you provide, *it will do you more harm than good.*

The other side of the coin is traditional publishing, which is how Rusty published his first book, and he had a great experience with it. For some people this is a good fit. If you're already a well-known person or have a widely known brand, traditional publishing may be the route you want to take. Likewise, if you're already a published author, you know your project is going to get attention, and therefore it makes sense to continue using traditional publishers.

Unfortunately, in today's publishing landscape, that may not be a realistic option for most people, as there are fewer and fewer traditional publishers, and most are raising the bar on what they will accept. All authors dream of getting agents who will go out and get them a $100,000 advance on their book. They'll get published, the publisher will promote and market the book, and they'll get rich. Then all they have to do is sit back and collect royalty checks.

That's pure fantasy. For most people, it just doesn't happen.

In fact, the majority of the titles that appear on the *New York Times* nonfiction best-seller list each year are those written by authors who had previously had a best-selling book or whose books have been on the list for a long time. The odds are stacked against you when it comes to breaking into that pool. It comes down to haves and have-nots. The ones who get the big contracts are often those who already have big names and an established track record with their brands and platforms.

Even if you do manage to get through the gates, there are three realities to be aware of with traditional publishing:

1. First, it takes an average of twelve to eighteen months to get published. That means you must have lots of patience—as well as a message that isn't incredibly time sensitive.

2. Second, the publisher owns the rights to the book, which can handcuff you in regard to what you can and can't do with the book or any of its content.

3. Finally, you need to consider how much your publisher is going to do to support the book. They will get it into book-stores perhaps, but they're likely going to rely on you to do most of the marketing. The books aren't going to sell them-selves, and, aside from unique cases, a traditional publisher isn't going to put a lot of money into promoting them for you unless they know there's a huge demand out there for it. In fact, your ability to promote the book to your platform is probably one of the reasons they bought the book from you!

We work with a lot of traditional publishers, and most do fantastic work, including the publisher of Rusty's first book. However, as noted, it's important to be aware that route isn't a fit for everyone.

The third route is independent publishing. That's where you engage a company that specializes in publishing and marketing your book. You hire them to create and publish a book that looks as good and reads as well as any you find on the shelves at Barnes & Noble. Then, when that's done, you have a partner that can help you make money using the book to grow your business. That's the goal most professionals have when they publish a book. To reach that goal, you want to work with someone who has experience working with CEOs and entrepreneurs to establish and market their authority status.

If you go this route, however, you have to understand that the primary aim of independent publishing is not to sell books. While some individuals will be able to have successful sales, the majority of authors who go this route will not. If you are interviewing an independent publisher and they are promising huge sales or leading you to that conclusion, you may want to reconsider that relationship. That doesn't mean you *won't* make money on the book—you can, just not in the way most people envision when they think of writing a book.

Think about it this way. You don't sell your book; your book sells you.

This is an idea that Andi Simon wholeheartedly agrees with. Here, she reveals how her books have helped her connect with exciting new client bases:

> My first award-winning book, *On the Brink: A Fresh Lens to Take Your Business to New Heights*, was published in 2016. Designed to tell the stories of eight clients who had been stuck, the book served to credential me and show others what they could expect when working with me. In 2021, my second award-winning book, *Rethink: Smashing the Myths of Women in Business*, was published. The stories of eleven successful women, *Rethink* pushed my own story forward. I was very interested in expanding my work to help women tackle the challenges of corporate life, address the work-life balance, and find ways to open and grow their businesses. *Rethink* allowed me to shift my speaking and host two successful virtual summits on *Rethinking Women*.

In each case, my motivation was to help spread the story I had been building over the years about how to embrace change. The impact was terrific. I was invited to conduct workshops and speak in Mexico three years after *On the Brink* was published. Many clients came to me with the book in their hands, asking if I could help them do the same as I had done for these clients.

The best independent publishers understand that for authorities, there are far better ways to make money with a book than by selling it. In fact, the worst way to make money off a book is by selling it.

Good ones teach you how to use your book as a marketing tool and deploy the authority it awards you to grow your business. The book serves as the foundation from which you can leverage media and generate leads. With the right

THE WORST WAY TO MAKE MONEY OFF A BOOK IS BY SELLING IT.

direction, doing this can give you an immeasurable advantage over your competitors. If done right, creating a book is an investment with exponential returns—but you have to go in with your eyes wide open on the outcome you are seeking.

To sum up, the most valuable thing about earned media like awards, media appearances, speaking engagements, etc. is the ability to remarket it moving forward. Nothing is as big a game changer to a skeptical audience as what someone reputable says about you. When they see brands they already respect being willing to credential you, it validates their decision to work with you and sets you and your business apart from competitors—because someone else they trust confirmed that you are indeed the right person to teach on this topic.

12

OWNED MEDIA

ONE OF THE REASONS we love using real estate as a backdrop for understanding the new media landscape is how perfectly it sums up the value proposition of each category of media.

When you reach an audience on earned or rented media, real estate that others own, they have all the leverage. You have to get their permission to reach that audience, whether by paying for it (advertising), playing by their rules (social media posts), or getting invited by them (PR, speaking, events, etc.) to communicate to their audience.

This isn't the case with your owned media because you fully maintain the connection to your audience, including your website, blog, email list, physical mailing list, and office space.

With media *you* own, *you* get to make all the rules. You control what it looks like, what message is communicated, what style you embody, and, most importantly, the way a relationship with your audience is started, nurtured, and converted into action.

WITH MEDIA *YOU* OWN, *YOU* GET TO MAKE ALL THE RULES.

A successful owned media strategy means thinking more like the media than a marketer. Media outlets are focused on attention and, more specifically, on doing everything they can to earn and then own the attention from their audience on an ongoing basis.

We want you to do exactly the same thing with your owned media strategy—and we're going to help you reach that objective in this chapter.

THE SHIFT FROM MACROMEDIA TO MICROMEDIA

As discussed, the biggest change that we have seen in the new media landscape is that the public is shifting attention away from large, generic mass media outlets and redeploying that attention to micromedia— created by individual authorities that are seen as both more trustworthy, more relevant, and often more entertaining, which leads to more value.

This shift is taking place for two primary reasons:

1. No matter what side of the aisle we are on, we increasingly question motives and angles on the information we get from major media—we just don't trust it anymore.

2. The ROI on time we give to large, generic media gives us a fractional return on the time we invest, because it's not nearly as niche as what we're able to get from micromedia.

The result of this is very good news for you: increasingly, your audience is looking to push major media out of the way and learn directly from you.

We hope this empowers you!

We have already talked at length in this book about how to create a great, mission-driven website and what kind of content strategy works best. Next, we're going to get specific about how to grow your owned media audience moving forward.

GROWING YOUR IMPACT BY BUILDING YOUR "AUTHORITY STADIUM"

The starting point for an owned media strategy is having a clear understanding of the three audiences that every business has in place at all times. To do this, we want you to visualize your owned media audience as an "Authority Stadium" that belongs to you. We are avid sports fans, so please indulge us as we use sports as a useful analogy in building your authority.

Picture a stadium filled with paid ticket holders. Picture tailgaters outside the stadium, connecting and taking in the fun. The folks inside the stadium are your clients, and the tailgaters are your known prospects—people you already have on your mailing lists or who are following you online but who haven't bought into your services yet.

We'll talk more about these groups in just a second. But first, there's one more audience group you want to be aware of—future fans. These are the people who fall into your target audience but who have no idea who you are. Future fans are outside the circle containing your audience that's already participating in your "game."

As we explain each group in turn, consider taking out a sheet of paper and writing your specific numbers in terms of the size of your current Paid Ticket Holders, Tailgaters, and Future Fans.

AUDIENCE 1: PAID TICKET HOLDERS. This first audience group includes your existing clients, strategic partners, and team members—everyone who has converted to the results you are trying to drive. For example, goals you might have for creating your Authority Advantage could include the following:

- Attracting and retaining clients

- Attracting and retaining talent

- Booking speaking engagements

- Generating donations to a nonprofit you support

- Selling books

Just like in a stadium, Paid Ticket Holders sit in different "sections" (some more expensive than others!) of your spectator zones. We encourage you to sort your Paid Ticket Holders into different sections based on the specific category they are in. Get a clear number on how many people are currently in each section. For example, if you have done twelve paid speaking engagements to date, you have twelve people in that section. If you have three hundred paying clients, put them in your client section. And so on.

After doing all your calculations, take a look: How many Paid Ticket Holders did you end up with? Which sections do you most want to grow in the future? We'll come back to this.

AUDIENCE 2: TAILGATERS. This second audience group sits outside the stadium and includes everyone on your email list or snail mail list (you "own" the connection to them) who has not yet decided to spend money with you, take that job offer, book you for a speech, or move forward with whatever conversion you may be trying to drive. In other words, they are a current fan and may even cheer for you, but they have not fully converted yet to pay to enter your stadium. Still, they *are* paying attention, and you have a chance to nurture them to the point they are ready to move forward—but you haven't established enough affinity with them to get them to buy a ticket.

Check your lists, and look at those who haven't done a transaction with you. How many people are in your Tailgater audience?

AUDIENCE 3: FUTURE FANS. This group is scattered far from your stadium and includes everyone who is squarely in your target audience—they could benefit tremendously from working with you or hearing your message—but they currently have no idea who you are.

In our experience, most marketing and advertising campaigns focus on reaching as many Future Fans (people who have never heard of you but could benefit from your product or service) as possible and then driving them back to a stadium (your website) where the only thing for them to do is either immediately move forward to Paid Ticket Holder status (where they buy something from you or sign up for some high-touch appointment like a free consultation), or if they are not yet ready to engage, they click the back button and head right back out of your stadium zone.

In other words, there's no tailgate in place to extend an interaction with that potential customer, team member or other target market because the website is only built as a virtual brochure where someone can either raise their hand to buy or request a meeting. But if they're not ready to do those things, there's really nothing else for them to do but hit the back button in their browser.

Shouldn't you be offering them more? Especially since you've gone to all the trouble to drive them there?

Here's what we mean by a "brochure website"—a site with all the usual tabs ("Mission Statement," "About Us," "Services," "Contact Page," etc.) that most have. Quite frankly, it does resemble a brochure as you continue reading through the text, looking at the pictures, and soaking it all in. It's a static, noninteractive experience—which is why we say there's not that much difference between that kind of website and a print brochure.

We want you to think about the last time you were handed a brochure at an event. You might have glanced through it; maybe the design even impressed you. However, if nothing motivated you to act on the information the brochure provided at that precise moment, you likely got out of view, tossed it in the trash, and forgot about it.

Similarly, if your website is set up like an online brochure, you're only converting the tiny percentage of site visitors who happen to reach your website at the precise moment they are ready to buy or contact you (think of this like a Hail Mary pass). All the other visitors are going to close the tab on their internet browser or hit the back button—essentially chucking your website aside just like they would a brochure.

This kind of approach—consistent with a marketing mindset—is the reason most advertising, PR, and marketing budgets go up almost entirely in smoke. You might have the best PR firm ever or be driving a huge number of clicks from that Facebook advertising campaign, causing people to flood toward your stadium. Which is wonderful.

But ... if you have a brochure website, where the only call to action is either to buy or to "contact us" for more information or a free appointment, it's pretty much the same as asking a cold lead to buy a ticket right away before you have built affinity with them. Few will pay the admission fee to enter your stadium.

Instead of trying to sell tickets right away, you should instead give them a reason to extend their interaction with you by joining your tailgate. After all, there's no obligation to hanging out in your "parking lot!" Future Fans, especially in this new media landscape, where skepticism is a way of life, are a lot more likely to take that short step rather than make the jump right away to becoming a Paid Ticket Holder.

When you reach people who are Future Fans, be it through a media interview, social media post, or other form of media, there are basically three things that can happen:

1. As noted, only a tiny percentage will be ready to buy immediately (far less than 1 percent on most campaigns).

2. A larger percentage will be intrigued and want to learn more—but aren't yet sure if you're the right person/product/service for their need.

3. An additional percentage will have no interest whatsoever.

When you have a *selling mindset* with your promotion, you are only set up to convert the first category: people ready to buy now. That kind of approach focuses on generating impressions and turning them into immediate purchases or inquiries for more information, which only provides value to the tiny number of people who are immediately ready to buy something. Again, it's the equivalent of a Hail Mary pass.

We can't overstate the importance of understanding this shift that has taken place and the opportunity it provides you as someone who wants to drive more leads and grow your business.

For years, marketing has been about immediate conversions. X number of brochures led to Y number of calls. X number of cold calls led to Y number of leads. X spent on advertising led to Y ROI. But the limiting factor on these "traditional" lead generation tactics is that they only allowed you to convert those people you happened to get lucky enough to reach on the right day when they were ready to buy. You had no opportunity to nurture that additional percentage of people you reached who were interested in your topic area but weren't ready to convert that day. As a result, you only got a fraction of the value from the money and time you spent on lead generation efforts.

By contrast, a *modern media mindset* focuses also (not *instead—* you're still converting those ready to buy) on extending the interaction by providing a mutually beneficial way for Future Fans to get value and learn more. This gives you a chance to nurture that contact and build an affinity over time, moving them down toward the field to head into the VIP Paid Ticket Holder section with fellow customers.

"TOURING" OTHER STADIUMS

How many people are in your stadium right now? How about your tailgate? A few hundred? Several thousand? If you did the exercise and now are a bit disappointed with the size of your current audience groups, we get it.

But let's remember something: *teams don't just play in their own stadiums.* They travel to other teams' stadiums and play there as well so that other audiences get a chance to see what they can do. That idea informs the next step of a savvy media mindset.

Any time you run a marketing or promotional campaign, whether it is a Facebook ad campaign, a radio advertisement, an NPR interview, or a speaking engagement, you reach an indirect audience on real estate that others own. When you do this, you're essentially standing on the field in a stadium where *they* play.

For example, if you write an article for Forbes.com, imagine you are standing on stage in a very big stadium that Forbes owns, one that is filled to the rafters with tens of millions of unique monthly visitors. When they publish your article, they have not only given you an implicit stamp of credibility; they have also given you a small sliver of their playing field. Your goal with that article is twofold:

1. To deliver great content

2. To give as many people as possible who read that article a reason to get up out of their seat in that Forbes stadium and follow you out the door to yours—in effect, driving them to your website or another call to action

When giving a speech, doing an interview, or writing an article, most people focus only on the first goal—to provide great content. Obviously, you must do that, but a systematic approach to lead generation doesn't end there. If you do what most people do, which is feature a bio that encourages people to "learn more" on their website, you may get lucky and have a few people follow you back to yours. But most people won't leave their seats because you haven't given them any reason to head "crosstown" to your stadium.

Instead, we want you to create a funnel that offers that audience in the Forbes stadium a clear, value-packed reason to motivate them to follow you to your tailgate. Typically, the starting point is your website. This is called a *lead magnet,* and some of you have been using versions of it for years to grow an owned media subscriber base.

CREATING A STRATEGIC MARKETING JOURNEY FOR FANS THAT WORKS

Few marketing tactics have become more popular in recent years than *funnels.* The term is thrown around by just about everyone, but few understand exactly what a funnel is and, more importantly, how to create one that performs at a high level. And although the term has become very popular, in our experience the typical sales funnel is too focused on transactional sales rather than on creating a long-term relationship that most authorities seek, which is why we prefer to think of it as a strategic marketing *journey*.

So … what is a strategic marketing journey?

In its most simple form, it's the journey a potential customer takes with you prior to buying. That journey is empowered by a system that you build, test, rebuild, and retest until you land on a predictable, high-quality ROI. Although most are digital marketing and lead generation tools, others focus purely on educating an audience to make a bigger impact.

Whether offline or online, a strategic marketing journey has five key steps:

1. Awareness

2. Lead magnet

3. Capture

4. Nurture

5. Sale or renurture

Not all customers who will buy from you require all five steps. Some leads, whether they are potential job applicants or customers, may become aware of you and jump right to step 5 because you got lucky enough to hit them on the right day or in the right state of mind (in other words, you successfully completed your Hail Mary pass). But this is the exception, not the rule, so you shouldn't build your strategy around that kind of long shot.

We want you to treat that kind of speedy conversion as icing on the cake but certainly not the core of your marketing conversion strategy. Instead, let's look at the different stages of crafting a journey that leads to the same goal.

STRATEGIC MARKETING JOURNEY STAGE 1: AWARENESS

Many think of stage 1 as all there is to marketing—generating awareness with those in your target market who don't know who you are. This can be done in a variety of different ways, including the following:

- Advertising
- Social media
- Direct mail
- Public relations
- Events
- Speaking
- Networking

The best way to generate awareness as it relates to your marketing journey is by providing value to your target audience in media that they respect and pay attention to. The more attention they give the outlet, the higher the volume and velocity of leads that will complete the journey you've created for them.

Again, successful lead generation within your journey means thinking more with a media mindset than a marketer's.

Media outlets are focused on getting the highest number of eyeballs—but, more specifically, on doing everything they can to earn and then own the attention from their audience on an ongoing basis. This is what a strategic marketing journey allows you to do—keep the attention of potential clients, talent, or partners by providing value and nurturing them toward a purchase or some level of engagement with you where they cross over into your Paid Ticket Holders. When you do this, you build affinity with your audience that motivates them to continue their journey with you.

We can't overstate the importance of creating a strategic marketing journey to give yourself a chance to go beyond that miniscule group that is ready to buy immediately. Otherwise, you end up wasting a lot of time and money on marketing that doesn't deliver the kind of results you're after, because you're constantly trying to throw that Hail Mary pass.

By contrast, a good journey backed by a media mindset focuses on extending the interaction with those in the Tailgater audience (interested, but not ready to buy). You do this by providing a mutually beneficial way for them to get value and learn more—giving you a chance to nurture that contact and build affinity over time. The starting point for keeping that group engaged with your journey is having a high-quality lead magnet in place.

STRATEGIC MARKETING JOURNEY STAGE 2: LEAD MAGNET

At the end of most media interviews, a consistent question is asked of the guest: "Where can our audience go for more information?"

This is a generous question because it gives the guest an opportunity to direct the audience wherever they want.

Most squander this opportunity by trying to drive the Hail Mary conversion with something like "You can head to my website and learn more about our services and reach out to schedule a free consultation." This works for the sub-1 percent that might be ready to take action—but what about the additional 10 to 20 percent who aren't ready to buy but are interested in learning more?

You must give them a way to dip their toe in the water with you and your content prior to getting to the point where they may be ready to buy. This kind of call to action is known as a lead magnet and essentially boils down to this: "What can I give you in exchange for your email address?" Once you understand what that is, they will become officially part of your tailgate.

We group lead magnets into one of three categories:

1. **NEWSLETTER SIGN-UP:** This first lead magnet is the most basic and (unfortunately) the most commonly used. It will often show up as offers such as "Click here to subscribe to our email newsletter" or "Click here to sign up for exclusive news and updates." As you might guess—or as you already know if this is your current lead magnet—this call to action converts at a horrific rate.

2. **FREE VALUE OFFER:** This typically shows up in one of the following ways: "Click here to download our whitepaper/e-book/workbook/free report." This second category converts better than the first one, but the limiting factor for those who don't yet have a brand established is that those who are landing on your website for the first time may not yet associate value with your content. This could limit success here.

3. **INTERACTIVE CONTENT:** This third category is the one that will give you the biggest return by far. Interactive content includes quizzes and assessments that give free, personalized value to website visitors (we touched on this in the chapter 11 section on speaking). Magazines have been using quizzes for years, but BuzzFeed was the first online platform to really

perfect the art of online interactive content. Books like Tom Rath's *StrengthsFinder 2.0*, Sally Hogshead's *How the World Sees You*, and Katty Kay and Claire Shipman's *The Confidence Code* leveraged high-value assessments to build email lists in the hundreds of thousands.

The magic of a good interactive online assessment, tool, or app is that it is the purest possible value exchange ensuring that *both* parties get value. Your audience gets free, personalized feedback based on the topic of the quiz. They might learn how they measure up to their peers in terms of retirement readiness, what kind of leaders they are, or what neighborhood best matches their personality—whatever type of assessment complements your content. Alongside individualized results, they get free, high-value content from you that helps them analyze those results.

Interactive content converts at a higher level than any other category that exists.

Most importantly for you, the leads, by using this interactive content, provide you with a large quantity of data on them that guides you on how to nurture them through your funnel. This kind of lead magnet can be incredibly powerful—both to inform and educate your audience and to grow your email list. But there are three key factors to be aware of:

1. Quizzes focused on the individual perform much better than those that assess a team or company.

2. The best quizzes have the clearest, simplest value proposition.

3. Perhaps most importantly, you must understand that a quiz/ assessment is not a survey. A survey is for your benefit— it collects lots of data and gives the survey taker the same generic response: "Thank you for participating in our survey"

(unless the survey benefits users with validation/views on how to view their core problems/opportunities). Generally, it's a one-way feedback mechanism that doesn't return actionable insights to the user. A great quiz/assessment provides a highly personalized response that includes not only the quiz taker's specific results but also context on how to interpret and learn from those results. You are prescribing a solution to your prospect at scale in a way that doesn't require any investment of time or resources apart from the initial setup.

It's rare to launch a lead magnet and have it immediately be a home run. You must be prepared to alter, update, revise, and even scrap lead magnets if they aren't working. As you get more sophisticated with your strategic marketing journey, you may even have multiple types of interactive content, each with its own lead magnets, in place at once to allow you to track which ones are performing and which aren't.

STRATEGIC MARKETING JOURNEY STAGE 3: CAPTURE

Many overlook this stage, but to us, it's the backbone to building a high-performing strategic marketing journey.

When you create the lead magnet that will anchor your strategic marketing journey, one of the most important questions to consider is this: "What kind of information do I need to capture about my prospect to best tailor the follow-up sequence to provide maximum value to them?"

The starting point here is to consider what characteristics make up a great lead for you. Is it

- title (decision maker),

- company revenue,

- number of employees,

- level of frustration with X,

- male or female, or

- age?

Each of you reading this has your own "wish list" of the attributes that define your perfect potential customer. Once you have that list in place, you need to work backward from it to weave in ways to pull that information from the potential client as part of your journey.

Obviously, it's nearly impossible to capture someone's information by just coming out and asking for it, but sometimes you can create a lead magnet with such value that you can create an "application" for it. This might be an application to attend a workshop, wine tasting, or "insider's only" summit, for example.

Most of the time, the best way to get this information is to utilize strategic questions. This is the other magic component of a good quiz within the context of lead generation. Strategic questions help you get key insights that allow you to determine if this is a good lead for your product or service. In other words, if you know that good prospects for your company have an annual revenue of between $1 million and $5 million, there should be a question in the quiz that asks how many employees that entrepreneur has. This is a less intrusive way to determine likely revenue. Whatever the one to three questions are that help you determine who's a good lead and who isn't, you want those embedded in your quiz so you can both capture and filter at scale.

In other words, you not only want to use the strategic marketing journey to grow your audience; you also want to know who should be in the front row of your stadium in terms of follow-up sequence versus who might be an upper-deck lead. The assessment allows you to do that.

One important note—just because someone doesn't answer the Trojan horse questions correctly doesn't mean it's not a valuable asset in your marketing funnel. As you grow your list, it will be made up of high-value leads and others who may not be buyers themselves but can help share and promote your content with others.

Ideally your lead magnet should be fully integrated with a CRM system that allows you to automatically sort leads into follow-up categories based on how they answer those questions. Some of the best systems for that are MailChimp, HubSpot, Infusion Soft, or Salesforce (which is the one we prefer). Your follow-up sequence, which we will discuss in the next part of this book, should be automatically triggered based on the information you capture from that lead in stage 3.

STRATEGIC MARKETING JOURNEY STAGE 4: NURTURE

Congratulations. You not only added a new Tailgater, but you also now have some data that allows you to serve them better on their journey to your stadium. But even though you have taken a major step toward lead generation success by capturing this lead, you now have to keep their attention, or they will wander off.

The only way to keep attention over time is to earn it consistently with high-quality content. That is why we spent so much time earlier in this book on how to organize your content strategy.

In addition to a general long-term content strategy that focuses on keeping attention, more sophisticated lead generation journeys will have a focused sequence of follow-up content and offers that give potential clients reasons to go ahead and buy.

For example, let's say you created a confidence quiz as a lead magnet to capture and convert toward an e-learning course. Here's how it might look:

STEP 1: Build awareness through targeted advertising.

STEP 2: Offer a free confidence quiz.

STEP 3: Capture name, email address, and minor demographic data via the quiz.

STEP 4: Begin nurture sequence by providing ...

1. Quiz results ...

2. ... followed one day later by a video further unpacking the category they fell in

3. ... followed two days later with a personalized invitation to join a free webinar on building confidence

   □ If they sign up for the webinar, trigger separate sequence (Zoom info plus a separate follow-up).

   □ If they don't sign up for the webinar, trigger five-week follow-up sequence focused on purchasing the book.

STEP 5: If they buy, drop out of the nurture sequence. If they don't buy, rinse and repeat.

The best thing you can do with your nurture sequence is provide value and then a very targeted, irresistible offer that accompanies it. If you're offering products that don't require your time and energy (e-learning, info products, etc.), then building a high-performing strategic marketing journey allows you to essentially build a virtual ATM. However, in most cases this takes lots of time and energy to perfect, and often the nurture sequence is that key differentiator between those that work really well and those that don't.

STRATEGIC MARKETING JOURNEY
STAGE 5: SALE OR RENURTURE

As we get more and more people into your tailgate, authority starts to play a bigger role in conversion rates. The more they see of your expertise and experience, the more they will begin to trust you.

At this stage, one of two things will happen.

If they move forward with a purchase and head into your stadium, your focus now becomes how you can empower them to talk about that purchase in a way that feels like they are winning. For example, if they buy a product from you, perhaps you might send them a personalized, signed copy of your book as a thank-you. That might surprise and delight them to the point that they want to share it on their LinkedIn profile or Facebook account ... which drives more people into the top of your funnel.

If they don't move forward with a purchase, then they become an ongoing part of your tailgate, and you can use the content strategy we discussed earlier to nurture them to the point they are ready to buy a ticket.

SHOULD YOU CONSIDER
A PODCAST?

"What is the one thing that, by my doing it, makes everything else easier or unnecessary?"

This exceedingly valuable question was the centerpiece of Gary Keller and Jay Papasan's masterpiece, *The One Thing*, which we were honored to help market during its launch several years ago. As leaders, we try to ask ourselves this question at every possible turn because it helps us focus on the high-leverage activity that reduces time spent and bends the curve on impact.

When it comes to content marketing (besides a book), we suggest that the one thing that, by you doing it, will make everything else easier or unnecessary is a podcast.

Why?

Your time is as valuable as it is scarce. If you have five to ten hours to devote personally to creating your Authority Advantage each month, a podcast is a good way to use half of that time for two reasons:

1. It gives you the best possible format for the interview series (Relationship-Driven content) that we have hammered as a primary focus throughout this book.

2. Content can flow from your podcast to every other channel you have (it posts to your blog, gives content for social media, etc.).

As we begin advocating for a podcast, we can sense a loud *but* swelling up inside you: "But it seems like everyone has a podcast ..."

That's not wrong. According to recent studies from Nielsen, Edison, and others, which we will further detail below, as of 2022 there were more than one million active podcasts and over thirty million episodes in more than a hundred languages.[8]

But ... (now it's our turn!) the reason to create a podcast isn't to become the biggest podcast in the country. Obviously, we want you to have as many listeners as possible, but that's a secondary goal to the relationship-building focus we want you to have.

---

8   Gavin Whitner, "Podcast Statistics (2022) – Newest Data + Infographic," musicoomph.com (Music Oomph, May 7, 2022), https://musicoomph.com/podcast-statistics/.

Podcasting has been around since the 1980s, making it one of the oldest forms of modern content marketing. The friction that prevented the current hockey stick–level growth in past years was the need to sit in front of a computer to listen to episodes.

In today's landscape, thanks to Bluetooth, smart speakers, mobile devices, and the meteoric rise of voice, it's as easy to listen to a podcast as it is to NPR or ESPN Radio, and that global accessibility, combined with the intersection with Relationship-Driven content, makes it more than worthy of your attention.

WHERE DOES PODCASTING FIT?

Although we have placed this topic in the owned media chapter, there is some debate as to whether podcasting falls into that category or is really rented media. The truth is that it really lives in both places.

The primary distribution points for podcasts are outside the mainstream media but really rented in nature, because Apple, Spotify, YouTube, and others own the audience that podcasts get distributed to.

At the same time, podcasts can also be directly distributed to an owned media audience and, as we discussed earlier in the book, can be a great format for Relationship-Driven content.

Based on the nature of podcast distribution lying outside major media, it creates a more level playing field for individuals and companies looking to compete for attention with the large generic media organizations that have previously enjoyed a monopoly on the airwaves.

If you look at current podcast rankings, it's likely you would see a combination of major media (like NPR), household names (like Dave Ramsey or Brené Brown), and even some names you may never have heard of who are reaching an audience at enormous scale through this medium.

A successful podcast can catapult you and your business into the limelight, but as you'll read about later in this section, we believe podcast success is tied much more to bottom-line results via guest relationships than the broader size of your audience.

But why not shoot for both?

According to recent studies from Nielsen, Edison, and others, here are some of the most important statistics to be aware of involving podcasts:[9]

- Business is the number two most popular podcast genre (behind society and culture).

- 75 percent of the US population has listened to a podcast.

- 37 percent of the US population listens to podcasts monthly.

- Podcast listeners are more active on every social media channel.

- Podcast listeners build brand affinity that drives them toward purchases.

How old are podcast listeners?

- Eighteen to twenty-four ~ 18 percent

- Twenty-five to thirty-four ~ 28 percent

- Thirty-five to forty-four ~ 21 percent

- Forty-five to fifty-four ~ 15 percent

- Fifty-five to sixty-four ~ 11 percent

- Sixty-five and over ~ 6 percent

These age statistics are compelling, but the most important data relates to the propensity for action that podcast listeners have along with their level of education and wealth. According to this same study, podcast listeners are 68 percent more likely to be postgraduates and 45 percent more likely to have an annual income of $250,000 and above.

That's an audience we suspect you're eager to reach.

---

9   Gavin Whitner, "Podcast Statistics (2022) – Newest Data + Infographic," musicoomph.com (Music Oomph, May 7, 2022), https://musicoomph.com/podcast-statistics/.

WHY PODCASTING?

We had the pleasure of working with Sally Hogshead on the launch of her second book, *How the World Sees You*. The follow-up to her debut title, *Fascinate*, it's a fantastic book that landed on the *New York Times* best-seller list and drove massive list building through the "Summer of Fascination" campaign surrounding her Fascination Advantage Assessment, which we highly recommend.

On the initial call we had with Sally to begin planning for the campaign, she said something that surprised us. She shared that she was less interested in the name-brand media that dominated her first campaign and much more interested in micromedia, because she had data that indicated micromedia drove most of the purchases in her first campaign.

Sally's Fascination Advantage Assessment gave her unique insight into which interviews, articles, or ads were actually driving results. Pound for pound, podcasts were providing the most engagement.

Why?

The reason podcasts tend to drive a higher percentage of activity is the level of relationship podcast listeners have with the host. Listening to a podcast is similar to hearing someone give a keynote speech. When you subscribe to a podcast and listen to it over time, it's akin to hearing a keynote speech in your car once a week. That kind of connection builds both trust and affinity on a level few other content media can.

Whether you decide to host your own podcast or just include them in a more intentional way in your outreach, it's important to respect the impact they can have on the growth of your audience.

PODCAST STRATEGY

A variety of podcast formats are available to you, but the best one in our experience is one that combines value for your audience with the kind of strategic relationship building that we discussed earlier in the book.

It's important to have two crystal clear goals in place when you start a podcast:

1. To build outbound relationships with individuals and companies that can help you grow your business

2. To build an audience of people who actively engage with your podcast, including empowering those who are already fans to share your content more

The second item is the harder thing to accomplish, but if you only achieve the first item, it's still a total and complete victory for your business. With that said, you can't just go through the motions with a podcast. You need to approach it as perhaps the most important content-marketing channel you have in place. A key part of that is being the best host you can be.

Many people who start a podcast have the mistaken belief that they need to embrace some kind of "radio host" persona they have in mind and typically end up coming off as inauthentic and formulaic. Do the complete opposite, and channel your inner Kindra Hall. If you're not familiar with Kindra, she's a best-selling author, keynote speaker, and storytelling authority who built a huge audience by being more of herself (we encourage you to check out her work at www.KindraHall.com for a great example of authentic authority). The reason your audience is going to stick with you over time is that they connect with *you*. Watch late-night TV talk shows? You probably choose one program over another because you like the host better. You may not even bother to check out who the guests are—because the host is who you connect with every single night.

Being a great host starts with being prepared for the interview. If you follow the process we're recommending, whether working with a company like ours to launch a Forbes Books Audio Podcast or utilizing your internal resources, much of the preparation will be done for you by a support staff member. Dig a bit deeper, and find a point of shared connection with your guest that opens the door to a deeper bond early in the interview. That might be a shared interest in college football, a mutual friend you found on LinkedIn, or a vacation spot they visited that you've also been to. If you can work that in early in the interview, you're going to endear yourself even more to that guest and likely set yourself up for a better interview.

Try to relax as much as possible, and know that your audience is going to enjoy the interview much more if they feel like a fly on the wall listening to an authentic, relaxed conversation between two authorities rather than something that feels like a scripted suit-and-tie style interview.

If possible, create an interview "war room" with a whiteboard where you can write the name of your guest, their book title, business name, and any other related information so that during the interview you're not shuffling around looking for those details.

PROMOTING YOUR PODCAST

As already noted, one of the best things about a podcast is that it gives you content that cascades across every other content-marketing channel you have.

Once a new episode is released, it's important to ensure you're getting maximum benefit from those sharing that link. To do so, instead of asking guests to share the link to iTunes, ask them to share the link to an individual blog post on your website where the interview is embedded. As a result, the audience will have a direct connection to your owned media—instead of sending them to real estate that Apple or another platform owns. Each podcast post should be accompanied by a text introduction, guest bio, key takeaways (click to tweet), and a call to action.

One important way to extend the reach of your podcast within social media is to share the link beyond LinkedIn, Facebook, or Instagram, whose algorithms, as we've noted, won't give much

ONE OF THE BEST THINGS ABOUT A PODCAST IS THAT IT GIVES YOU CONTENT THAT CASCADES ACROSS EVERY OTHER CONTENT-MARKETING CHANNEL YOU HAVE.

love to an external link. Instead, shoot a quick one-to-two-minute video with your takeaways from that episode. You can call it a preview and then use that as native content to give your podcast episodes extra reach when you share them.

You also want to make life as easy as possible on both your audience and your guest in terms of sharing the link with their audience. One of the best ways to do this is to have a consistent graphic in place that you can update with the episode number and image of your guest. It needs to be well designed so your guest is excited to share it.

Although Apple has largely owned discoverability for podcasts through its iTunes app, with the growth of Amazon Alexa and Google Home, discoverability is now happening in a more fragmented environment. As a result, you need to be sure to distribute your podcast across each of these channels.

BUILDING YOUR PODCAST GAME PLAN

If you haven't been a big podcast listener up to now, the first step is to download a few podcasts and begin listening to get a feel for what works well and what doesn't. The best way to find good ones is to search through the rankings on iTunes or Podbay.fm and find the top-ranked podcasts in your topic area. If possible, listen to a combination of highly produced podcasts from outlets like NPR as well as podcasts from individual authorities you may not have heard of—you're likely to learn much more about what works from the latter category.

Once you get a feel for podcasts as a medium, begin considering what resources you're going to need in place to make it possible. We talked earlier in this section about the logistics involved with scheduling, editing, and distributing a podcast. You can either hire for those, or a company like Forbes Books can help, but you will still need the right equipment.

If you decide to build a visible studio in your office or building lobby, you're going to need more than the standard level of equipment we list below. If you're going to facilitate a virtual podcast in which you interview guests wherever they may be, you'll need a mic (Heil makes very good ones), preamps (Scarlett makes very good ones), and recording software (we use ECamm Call Recorder).

As mentioned earlier, don't put too much pressure on yourself to be perfect—a good podcast is informal in terms of the content and high quality in terms of the final product from a sound quality perspective. It is our belief that the right podcast can be the best business development tool that exists for your company and is the definition of best and highest use when it comes to time that you personally put into building your Authority Advantage.

BEGIN WITH THE END IN MIND

As we close out this chapter, we want to emphasize that your strategic marketing journey doesn't have to be perfect or even overly sophisticated. We feel the need to say that because a lot of leaders hold off on building a strategic marketing journey because they think they aren't experienced enough with digital marketing to create one that works. However, the more important piece of building a big tailgate is providing value to your audience

Finally, we cannot overemphasize the importance of owning as much of the real estate for your tailgate as possible (owning your media and your audience). In this new media landscape, technology is a double-edged sword—either it can allow you to create leverage by building a direct connection with your audience or it can allow others to insert themselves between you and your target audience. At all times we want you focused on two things: 1) serving your audience with great content, and 2) working them toward your stadium with a clear, elegant next step that moves them toward your owned media.

Perhaps the best advice we can give you is this: however you choose to use media, always *begin with the end in mind.*

HOWEVER YOU CHOOSE TO USE MEDIA, ALWAYS BEGIN WITH THE END IN MIND.

No matter what you use to build your Authority Advantage, be it a podcast, book, blog, and/or videos, you should have an endgame in mind. Whenever we talk with business leaders about the impact of building their Authority Advantage, we like to ask how they will measure success.

Most people intuitively understand how an authority brand can benefit them, but many don't have an exact idea of how they're going to measure their success along the way. Very often success and failure are more subjective and instinctive than they are objective or data driven. It's important to resist the magnetism of the subjective route and instead create hard metrics that can be put up on a board to gauge the success of your authority-building efforts.

For some individuals, metrics do not matter. People have different motivations and goals for pursuing an Authority Advantage. For some it could be making an impact or advancing a cause. In instances like these, success isn't always based on a black-and-white metric. That's fine, but you need to be clear about that up front. However, for most people, pursuing an Authority Advantage is a route to growing a business and freeing up more time to spend with their family or to pursue personal interests. To gauge that kind of success, you need to have concrete metrics and know exactly what you're aiming for.

Beginning with the end in mind is rule number two from Stephen Covey's iconic book, *The 7 Habits of Highly Successful People.* It's undeniably true; the most successful people start with a vision of what they want the end to look like. We believe this should be emphasized whenever any professional undertakes this kind of initiative. You must know what success looks like and where you want to end up. If you don't, how will you know if you're happy with the results?

Once you have your end goal in mind, you can use that to create your specific MAP in such a way as to help you reach that desired end. This MAP should have checkpoints along the way to make sure you're tracking toward your desired end goal. We have seen many a journey veer off course. Only those who set unemotional, data-driven benchmarks have the clarity to swerve back onto the road.

For example, perhaps one of your goals is to use your enhanced authority status to generate five new clients in the first year. As we have discussed throughout this book, it can take time to build a large audience of Paid Ticket Holders or even fill your tailgate audience, but along the way you can leverage your content marketing to work toward that specific objective. For example, you can use Relationship-Driven content on your blog as an engine to build relationships with potential clients. Writing a blog (and most certainly a book) becomes a tool to expand your network. Featuring key individuals or companies on your blog or your book presents huge opportunities. Those companies and individuals will more readily promote both if they're featured by you.

But if you don't have clarity on what you're looking to get out of the authority-building process, then you will likely end up spending a lot of time on efforts that may end up off target, and those can have huge financial consequences. On the flip side, if you work backward from your end goal, you may be like many authorities who see immediate and substantial returns on their time and investment because of the business development impact they are able to make.

Knowing what success looks like for you and what metrics you will use to gauge it means you can work toward them from the very start. Although big picture goals can be similar, the vision is different for everyone, and there is no right or wrong answer. We always say that authority is firmly based on what industry, business, marketplace, and community you are in. Those factors and the goals you have for your business and industry are going to determine which pieces of the framework we have laid out in this book you should be concentrating on.

If you want to get more specific about what your MAP should look like, we're happy to help with that.

OPTIMISTIC FUTURE • LEARNING AND GROWING • CONTROL OVER YOUR DESTINY • EARNED SUCCESS • QUALITY RELATIONSHIPS •

HAPPINESS AND AUTHORITY

IS THERE A CONNECTION between creating an Authority Advantage and happiness? Can following an authority-building path actually lift your life satisfaction?

If you ask people what they want out of their lives—or what they want out of their careers, for that matter—the most common answer you would hear is "I want to be happy." That raises the following question: "What is happiness?" What is this illusive concept most people seem to spend their lives chasing?

The truth is that just like success, happiness means different things to different people. There is no commonly accepted definition of happiness that applies to everybody. It can be difficult to create a road map to happiness when it's a different destination for each person. In fact, some people couldn't even tell you where that place would be for them.

IF WE KNOW WHAT DRIVES HAPPINESS, THEN WE KNOW WHAT THINGS WE NEED TO FOCUS OUR ATTENTION AND TIME ON.

So, over the course of our careers as entrepreneurs, we have tried to really invest time to determine the answers to these questions: "What is happiness, and what drives it?" If we know what drives happiness, then we know what things we need to focus our attention and time on. Over our own careers, we've settled on five major drivers of happiness:

1. **LEARNING AND GROWING**. There's a saying you've probably heard: "You're either growing, or you're dying." There is no such thing as merely staying the same. On this journey, you are either progressing or digressing. The people who are constantly learning and growing are more fulfilled than people who are not. Learning and growing as an individual may mean acquiring new skills, reading new books, teaching yourself a new vocation, or elevating existing knowledge. People who are focused on professional and personal development tend to be the happiest and most content. This driver of happiness is so powerful that it has become the mission statement of EO, a group we're both proud to be members of.

2. **HAVING CONTROL OVER YOUR DESTINY**. There's nothing more hopeless and discouraging for people than feeling that

no matter what effort they put forth, the outcome has already been decided. When you build an Authority Advantage, you give yourself leverage to decide how you want to spend your time and where you want to make your impact. Even if you are in a situation that doesn't directly tap into your passions, building an audience and creating media you own allows you to build a bridge to where you want to go.

3. **EARNED SUCCESS**, or goal attainment. There is something about earning success that is personally more satisfying and rewarding than just getting something without working for it. Recall a class you took in high school or college where you had to struggle a bit. Maybe you studied every night and joined study groups. You applied yourself and invested a lot of time to understanding the material. Then the big test came, and you aced it! That probably gave you a tremendous feeling of success and satisfaction. On the other hand, think of a class where you literally could have slept through it and *still* aced the test. If you don't have to apply yourself at all, getting an A won't give you anywhere near the level of satisfaction you'd get from the class you worked hard to master. In other words, not all As are equal. When you earn success, you are proud and fulfilled. When you're simply given something, there is no fulfillment. If anything, it creates a sense of entitlement. There is no getting around it: earning success and achieving goals are huge drivers of happiness.

4. **QUALITY RELATIONSHIPS**. These are not just your professional relationships but important relationships in every facet of your life. Perhaps it's with your parents, your spouse or significant other, your children, your colleagues, or your

friends. Whatever relationships mean the most to you, it's important to foster them with time and attention. The more quality relationships people have in their lives, the happier they tend to be. We've seen it time and time again. When you have strained and conflicted relationships, whether it's with parents, your boss, or the couple living across the street, it creates friction and frustration. It creates anger and stress— even sadness. All these feelings are the antithesis of happiness.

5. **HAVING AN OPTIMISTIC FUTURE**. This means you are hopeful about what's to come. When you stop having things to look forward to, you might as well hang it up. Perhaps it's looking forward to having an independent life or getting into the career of your dreams. Maybe it means falling in love and getting married. Later, maybe it could be about having children; most parents will say that is one of the greatest joys of life. When the children are grown, there are grandchildren to look forward to. Or *whatever* it is that puts a smile on your face when you look forward to it. Elvis Presley once said, "I believe the key to happiness is someone to love, something to do, and something to look forward to." And we're not here to argue with "the king."

So, in our cases, anyway, these five things—learning and growing, having control over your destiny, earning your success, developing quality relationships, and being optimistic about your future—are drivers of happiness. What's really interesting to us is, as we've looked at our paths in becoming authorities and investing in creating our Authority Advantage, we realized we were actually supporting and growing our happiness as well!

In a nutshell, we contend that investing time and resources in building your Authority Advantage by making a commitment to becoming a leader and expert in your field will make you a happier person. If you need more convincing, let's start peeling back the layers.

LEARNING AND GROWING

If you were the authority in your field—the expert when it came to your product or service—you would have to constantly apply yourself and constantly sharpen your sword. The experts of today will not be those of tomorrow unless they continue to learn, grow, and adapt with the changing marketplace and world we live in. You may have been the smartest tech expert in the year 2000, but if you haven't constantly learned and grown since then, by 2022 (and probably much earlier), you would have been left in the dust. When you make a commitment to be an authority, it's a commitment to lifelong learning and growing.

CONTROL OVER YOUR DESTINY

Being the go-to authority gives you more choices, and the more choices you have, the more control over your destiny you have. Wealthy or poor, everyone has problems. In fact, wealthy and poor people share many of the same problems—the difference being that wealthy people have more options and more choices on how to deal with those problems. Similarly, when you become the expert and an authority, you also have more options. You're a person who is now in higher demand, giving you the ability to choose which engagements fulfill you. You're someone whom people now listen to when you speak. You're an individual who now has more influence—someone who is seen as a trusted advisor, not as a salesperson peddling goods. All of which gives you more control over your destiny and that of your company.

EARNED SUCCESS

Becoming an authority and being seen as a thought leader, unfortunately, doesn't happen overnight. There is no magic pill. There is no potion or formula that will instantly turn you into an authority. And although that's what so many of us might think we want, we would argue that the journey you undertake in becoming an authority is more satisfying than the destination. The person you must become to be the go-to leader and expert in your field will give you pride and fulfillment that can last a lifetime. As you embark on this authority-building journey—which will take time—the things you do and the person you will have to become to be worthy of commanding thought leadership will take significant work. That is the definition of earned success. That is attainment of goals. Perhaps your goal is to be featured in *Forbes* or to be a regular contributor on CNBC. Perhaps you want to be invited to keynote the largest industry conference your company participates in. All these things are goal attainment, and authority can help you attain those goals as well as help you stand out from your competitors. Patti Brennan sums it up nicely:

> The differentiation is me coming forward and wanting to make a difference first, in whatever way that looks like. It could be reading my book, it could be listening to the podcast, reading my social media posts, or getting my quarterly letters. And whether it's somebody off the street or a client, all of this combines to say, "Hey, you should listen to this lady. She really knows what she's talking about. And she's different because she cares, because she's giving us all this stuff completely for free." I've always believed that we don't work with money—we work with people.

QUALITY RELATIONSHIPS

You can easily see the logic in what we've been saying so far—but how in the world does building an Authority Advantage help you create more quality relationships? At first, it may not seem obvious. However, there are two reasons this is the case. The first gets back to the media mentality: if you give value first without any expectation of reciprocation, you become someone who attracts opportunities and good people.

Additionally, we would argue that the more authority you have in your position, the more desirable you are to other people. There's a famous adage that if you put a sign up along the side of the road that says, "Free Puppies," nobody will stop. But if you put a sign up that says, "Puppies $500," many will want to stop and take a look. As you become an authority, as you grow increasingly significant, more people are going to want to participate in your orbit. Old marketing pro (and our friend) Dan Kennedy likes to say, "The higher up in the food chain you go, the more you are paid for who you are rather than what you do." Think about that for a minute: *the more you are paid for who you are rather than what you do.* Well, who can pay more? Often the person who can pay more is a strategic relationship or customer. The more you become an authority, the higher level your sphere of influence and the higher level of circles you begin to run in. That results in higher-level relationships. Believe it or not, we've had authors tell us that becoming authorities in their fields changed their relationships for the better—including those with their families and loved ones.

OPTIMISTIC FUTURE

Our final driver of happiness, an optimistic future, can also be supported through authority. When you become the go-to thought leader, when you have a line of people wrapped around your office wanting to work with you, when you have a clamoring group of people in line to talk to you after you give a speech or a presentation, not only is it fun but it makes you a magnet for opportunity. The more opportunities you have in your life, the more optimistic you become about the future, and the more you can help others—leading to a more prosperous and fulfilling life.

As we conclude this book, we want to put the focus on why everything we have talked about really matters.

Yes, it's meant to give you a MAP to build and market your authority so you can have a competitive edge in your field, industry, or location and make a bigger impact. However, success is only a means to an end. The true goal that most people seek to obtain is happiness. When we consider that and look at these major drivers of happiness, it tells us something about the real power of creating your own Authority Advantage. We believe taking the journey down this road will be the greatest and most fulfilling decision you can make for your future.

And there has never been a better time than *now*! The world is changing, and the media landscape is continuing to shift. The power that has traditionally belonged to corporate media giants is now in the hands of every individual for the benefit of anyone who understands how to use it. Now *you* know how to use it to build trust at scale.

In the past only sovereign powers or mainstream media could confer authority. Today, we live in an era when individuals can confer their own authority by serving others first. By doing so, business owners, entrepreneurs, executives, and thought leaders can gain an outsized advantage on their competition, increase the speed of trust with their customers or clients, and leverage success into greater success.

You now have the knowledge to start leveraging the new media landscape to your advantage. You understand how to develop your Authority MAP and how to implement it.

Success looks different to everyone, which is why the Authority Advantage works so well. It's customizable, adaptable, and authentic to who you are and what you do. Whatever means success for you, we hope the road map we have provided here can help support you on the way.

To your success,

Adam and Rusty

For current resources, visit our website at:

BOOKS.FORBES.COM/AUTHORITY-RESOURCES

RESOURCES

A WELCOME GIFT

Download Adam and Rusty's e-book, *Authority Marketing*, for free. In this book, you will explore the seven foundational pillars of Authority Marketing, including why thought leadership is your most important secret weapon to grow business, attract opportunity, and make competition irrelevant.

OUR FRESHEST INSIGHTS

Access the best tools and ideas for leaders who want to build authority in their field on our blog.

TAKE THE ASSESSMENT

Find out your Authority Status: Are you sought after for your expertise, an influencer for leaders in your field, or a novice looking to expand your reach?

OTHER RESOURCES

- *The Definitive Guide to Publishing Your First Book: For Entrepreneurs, Business Moguls, and CEOs* clearly and carefully explains the book publishing process for professionals.

- *Our Welcome Guide* outlines everything you want to know about Authority Media and Publishing Programs at Forbes Books plus how-to articles and examples of more than fifteen authors who have leveraged a book to open doors and build their Authority.

APPLY TO BE OUR NEXT FORBES BOOKS AUTHOR

Forbes Books is for leaders who truly are the best in business in their field and want to share their knowledge and passion to make an impact. Join an exclusive community limited to those who apply and meet certain criteria and elevate your success to significance. **BOOKS.FORBES.COM/APPLY**

GET IN TOUCH

Call us at **843-414-5600** or email us at **INFO@FORBESBOOKS.COM**

WE WISH YOU ALL THE BEST ON YOUR JOURNEY TO CONTINUED SUCCESS!

ABOUT THE AUTHORS

ADAM WITTY

Adam Witty is the founder and CEO of Forbes Books, the book publishing brand of Forbes Media, publisher of *Forbes*. What began in the spare bedroom of his home is now one of the most respected independent business book publishers in the world with more than two thousand authors in forty-four US states and fourteen countries. Founded in 2005, Advantage Media publishes under namesake Advantage Books and provides public relations, podcast, digital media, and serialized content services to CEOs, entrepreneurs, and leaders. In 2016, Advantage and Forbes partnered to create Forbes Books.

Adam was listed on the prestigious Inc. 30 Under 30 list of America's Coolest Entrepreneurs in 2011. Advantage has been named on the Inc. 500/5000 list for six of the past eight years. Adam is the author of five books and has appeared in *USA Today*, *Investor's Business Daily*, *Wall Street Journal*, and on ABC and FOX. Adam is a leading global expert on "Authority Media" and coauthored the best-selling book *Authority Marketing*. Adam also coauthored *Book the Business:*

How to Make Big Money With Your Book Without Even Selling a Single Copy with marketing legend Dan Kennedy. Adam's most recent book, *Relentless Implementation*, was coauthored with Alan Mulally, retired CEO of Boeing Commercial Airplanes and Ford Motor Company.

Adam is the Publisher of *Forbes Books Review Magazine*. Adam is an Eagle Scout, member of EO, YPO, and past Board Chair of Clemson University's Spiro Entrepreneurship Institute and nonprofit Youth Entrepreneurship South Carolina. Adam is a commercial pilot with instrument and seaplane ratings. Adam was named Charleston's 2019 Entrepreneur of the Year by the Harbor Entrepreneur Center.

Adam, wife Erin, and son Ellis are proud to call Charleston home. Their "grumpy cat" Pecan Pie is often confused with Garfield.

You can reach Adam at awitty@forbesbooks.com or learn more at AdamWitty.com or books.forbes.com.

RUSTY SHELTON

Rusty Shelton first spoke at Harvard on the changing world of marketing and PR at the age of twenty-three.

He is a best-selling author, dynamic keynote speaker, and successful entrepreneur who has focused his career on helping leaders build thought leadership focused on impact, not ego. Rusty wrote three acclaimed books and speaks around the world to a variety of audiences, from YPO to Forbes. He is Founder & Chairman of Zilker Media, an award-winning agency based in Austin, Texas, that builds people-driven brands and a strategist at Forbes Books.

Rusty's keynotes blend humor and targeted examples to challenge assumptions about personal branding. He's known for a mix of storytelling; candor; and practical, put-it-into-action-next-week guidance, showing leaders how to make an impact and build trust in an increasingly skeptical world and have a lot of fun along the way.

He has shared the stage with Steve Forbes and Alan Mulally, spoken for YPO, EO, SXSW Interactive, the University of Texas, numerous Fortune 1000 companies, and served on the faculty at more than twenty Harvard Medical School CME courses.

He is the coauthor (alongside Adam Witty) of *The Authority Advantage: Building Thought Leadership Focused on Impact, Not Ego* (ForbesBooks, 2023), *Authority Marketing: How to Leverage 7 Pillars of Thought Leadership to Make Competition Irrelevant* (ForbesBooks, 2018), and coauthor (alongside Barbara Cave Henricks) of *Mastering the New Media Landscape: Embrace the Micromedia Mindset* (Berrett-Koehler, 2016).

An avid Texas Longhorns fan, he sits on the Texas Exes PR Committee and is a proud member of Entrepreneurs' Organization (EO) in Austin, where he serves on the board.

He lives just west of Austin in Spicewood with his wife, Paige, three children (Luke, Brady, and Sadie), and their very rowdy black lab, Charlie. Rusty loves to play golf, fish, and coach his sons' sports teams, and he is the QB for Lake Travis' top "old man" flag football team.

You can reach Rusty at rusty@zilkermedia.com or learn more at www.RustyShelton.com or www.ZilkerMedia.com.

ACKNOWLEDGMENTS

ADAM WITTY

First, I want to thank the people that have made this book possible.

To my coauthor, business partner, and friend Rusty Shelton, you are prolific, patient, and a fabulous marketing teacher. I love collaborating with you.

To the talented professionals at Forbes Books that directly supported this project, your skill and professionalism have made this book what it is. Thank you to Mindy Cordell, Joel Schettler, Joel Canfield, Laura Rashley, Heath Ellison, Wesley Strickland, Matthew Morse, Steve Elizalde, Corrin Foster, and Beth LaGuardia. You have my deepest admiration and appreciation.

Second, I want to thank the people that have made me who I am.

To my beautiful bride, Erin, and son, Ellis, you mean the world to me and are my biggest supporters. To my parents, John and Susan Witty, thank you for leading by example and creating a terrific foundation.

Deep thanks to all of my teammates at Advantage Media and Forbes Books for making each day a joy and working together to grow entrepreneurs and businesses to benefit mankind. Special thanks to our incredible supporters Scott Manning, Verne Harnish, Andrew Sherman, Mark Richardson, David Meerman Scott, and Clint Greenleaf.

Finally, I want to express my gratitude to mentors Pat Williams, Dan Kennedy, and Alan Mulally who have taught so much for over twenty years.

I've tried to live my life by a simple motto: "You only live life once, but if you work it right, once is enough." I am grateful to the many people that have had such a positive impact on my life and encouraged me to share, serve, and give. With God's grace, I'll have more to give.

RUSTY SHELTON

I have lived a very blessed life and have been so fortunate to receive so much love, wisdom, and support from so many through the years.

I have to start by thanking my wife Paige for her love and grace— my list of blessings always starts with you. Thank you for all you give to me and our family. Life is so fun and rewarding with you.

Thanks to our oldest son, Luke, for making your old man so very proud. You are a natural born leader and are destined for so many great things in your life. I'm looking forward to watching you conquer the world. Keep fishing, building, and pursuing your dreams. I'm excited to support you each step of the way.

To our youngest son, Brady, for his blend of humor, kindness, and emotional intelligence—you are such a blessing to everyone around you, and you make your mom and me so very proud. Thanks for being by my side for golf, football, fishing, and many an adventure. I'm looking forward to so many memories with you in the future as you make your mark. Big things are ahead.

And to our only daughter, Sadie, for being an answered prayer and a bright light to all around you. Your spirit is so vibrant, and I can't wait to watch you make your mark on this world. Your mom and I are so thankful for you and we're excited about the bright future ahead of you.

I'd like to thank my parents, Walt and Roxanne, for being my foundation and giving me so much through the years. Dad has always been my role model and has been such a valuable guide in my life. My mom has molded so much of who I am and is such a blessing to all of those around her and certainly me. Thanks for being the best parents a Texas boy could have ever asked for. You inspired so much confidence in me.

Thanks to my sister, Courtney, for being the most courageous woman I know. You impact so many people with your work but what stands out to me is what a remarkable mom, sister, and wife you are. I'm so lucky to be your brother. And thanks to my brother-in-law, Chad, who has become a brother to me. I'm more thankful for you than you know.

I'd like to thank my Zilker Media family, beginning with my partner and Zilker Media CEO Paige Velasquez Budde. You are the most naturally gifted leader I know, and it's been such an honor to watch you really lean into that gift over the past few years. It's a blast working with you, sharing the stage, and having fun with you and Jordan, and I'm excited about a lot of fun ahead as we keep building the best agency around. Thanks to my mentor and Zilker Media partner Clint Greenleaf for opening many doors for me in my life and career. I appreciate you. And to the L team: from Patti Conrad (the wolf!), who keeps me on track and out of our trouble, to Shelby Janner, who both believed in and helped set the vision for the agency (and is a total rockstar), to Nichole Williamson, who makes me laugh and is becoming one hell of a leader herself. And to the broader Zilker Media team, I'm so grateful to each of you and excited to be on this ride together.

I'd like to thank my coauthor and good friend Adam Witty for being such a fantastic partner on this book and in business. You have opened many doors for me, including ones you didn't have to, and I'm both grateful and excited about what we'll accomplish together in the future.

To the Forbes Books team, including Mindy Cordell, Laura Rashley, Matthew Morse, Wesley Strickland, Joel Schettler, Joel Canfield, Steve Elizalde, Corrin Foster, and all others involved in the creation of this book, thank you for your endless patience and expertise as you helped Adam and me create a book that we hope will impact a lot of lives. And to the broader Forbes Books team that I have had the pleasure of working with over the past seven years—so much talent and so much team work, and it's been my honor to build relationships with so many of you as we have worked together to grow this great company. Thank you.

To my partner and friend Nick Alter for challenging me and working alongside me to make an impact and grow great companies.

And to mentors that have helped me through the years, from Mike Odom to Robbie Vorhaus to my coauthor and friend Barbara Cave Henricks—thank you for investing in me.

NOTES